American Pope

American Pope

Scott Hahn and the Rise of
Catholic Fundamentalism

SEAN SWAIN MARTIN

◆PICKWICK *Publications* • Eugene, Oregon

AMERICAN POPE
Scott Hahn and the Rise of Catholic Fundamentalism

Copyright © 2021 Sean Swain Martin. All rights reserved. Except for brief quotations in critical publications or reviews, no part of this book may be reproduced in any manner without prior written permission from the publisher. Write: Permissions, Wipf and Stock Publishers, 199 W. 8th Ave., Suite 3, Eugene, OR 97401.

Pickwick Publications
An Imprint of Wipf and Stock Publishers
199 W. 8th Ave., Suite 3
Eugene, OR 97401

www.wipfandstock.com

PAPERBACK ISBN: 978-1-6667-3116-3
HARDCOVER ISBN: 978-1-6667-2334-2
EBOOK ISBN: 978-1-6667-2335-9

Cataloguing-in-Publication data:

Names: Martin, Sean Swain, author.

Title: American pope : Scott Hahn and the rise of Catholic fundamentalism / Sean Swain Martin.

Description: Eugene, OR: Pickwick Publications, 2021 |Includes bibliographical references.

Identifiers: ISBN 978-1-6667-3116-3 (paperback) | ISBN 978-1-6667-2334-2 (hardcover) | ISBN 978-1-6667-2335-9 (ebook)

Subjects: LCSH: Hahn, Scott | Catholic Church—Doctrines | Theologians | Religious fundamentalism | Fundamentalism—Controversial literature.

Classification: BX1751.3 M37 2021 (paperback) | BX1751.3 (ebook)

09/29/21

For my parents, Jim and Sue Martin,
and their steadfast conviction that love and kindness is
is greater than rightness.

And for Beth, Gwen, and Milo my world and my home.

Whoever takes refuge in fundamentalism is afraid of setting out on the road to truth. He already "has" the truth, and deploys it as a defense, so that any questioning of it is interpreted as an aggression against his person.

Discernment, on the other hand, allows us to navigate changing contexts and specific situations as we seek the truth. Truth reveals itself to the one who opens herself to it.

–Pope Francis, *Let Us Dream*

Contents

Acknowledgments ix

Introduction xi

1 | The Life and Thought of Scott Walker Hahn 1

2 | Revelation's Gift of the Mass 27

3 | Benedict the Inerrantist? 56

4 | The Fundamentals of a Truly Catholic America 84

Bibliography 113

Acknowledgments

BEFORE CONTINUING, I WOULD like to acknowledge those who have assisted me in this project. First and foremost, this book would not exist in any fashion without the tireless, patient, and compassionate encouragement and guidance of my mentor, Dr. William Trollinger. I will be forever grateful for the hours that he has spent over the past several years sitting down with me to ensure not only that the dissertation on which this book is based was completed but also that it remained mine. He has always encouraged me that it is my voice that is needed in regards to this topic and he has worked endlessly to help unearth that voice, chipping away graduate student doubts and anxiety. His friendship, guidance, and mentorship have been one of the most powerful acts of charity and selflessness that I have ever experienced, and I am eternally changed by it. He is the scholar I aspire to be.

Along with my mentor, I would like to thank Drs. Sandra Yocum, Silviu Bunta, Meghan Henning of the University of Dayton, and Randall Stephens of the University of Oslo. That they were willing to sacrifice their time and attention to work with me on this project is humbling and inspiring. I will not ever be able to adequately express my gratitude and indebtedness for their assistance and guidance in bringing the rough ideas of this project into the form it is now. Anything praiseworthy in this project belongs to my committee and my director. Any mistakes or failings that remain are mine alone.

I would also like to extend my gratitude to my brother, Jay Martin, and sister-in-law, Jennifer Newsome Martin, both of Notre Dame, as well as David Wheeler-Reed, whose friendship and support yielded countless hours of conversation and advice, without which I would have been lost. I am extremely grateful to Dr. Susan Trollinger for being willing to assist with parts of my second chapter and for her championing my project among her students. I also need to thank my good friends, Nick Mayrand and Steve Joebgen, for writing sessions, conversations, writing breaks, and constant companionship. I would be remiss, indeed, to not also express my gratitude to my wife, Beth Martin, my mother, Sue Martin, and my sister-in-law, Allison Meiners, for their proofreading and editing support. My time in the Religious Studies Department at the University of Dayton has proved unquestionably to be one of the most important decisions of my professional career and I am so thankful for the six years of kindness, guidance, education, and friendship that I have been offered by staff and faculty alike, particularly Drs. William Portier, Brad Kallenberg, and Vince Miller, and the tireless and saintly Amy Doorley. I am also thankful to the graduate student community in the Religious Studies Department at the University of Dayton, particularly, Laurie Eloe, Anthony Roselli, Tyler Campbell, Scott Howland, Michael Romero, Josh Wopata and Jens Mueller. I could not imagine a better cohort with whom to be on this journey. I also would like to extend my gratitude to Cincinnati's Muse Cafe for providing a comfortable environment (and particularly strong coffee) in which to write, and the Glass Cannon Podcast, who traveled with me on this journey through endless hours of distraction and entertainment while I wrote this work over these past few years.

I will never be able to properly convey everything my wife and daughter have meant to me during this time. Beth has provided me with endless support and love during what have been the most demanding, incredible, difficult, heartbreaking, and inspiring years of my life. My daughter, Gwen, has brought a light into my life that I never imagined possible and her simple love and affection has carried me through every day since she entered our lives. I would be nothing without them and everything in my life and career I devote to them. And for my family, especially my parents, Jim and Sue Martin, and in-laws, Steve and Sharon Meiners, who have never stopped believing in me, supporting me, and praying for me, I am more and more thankful every day.

Lastly, I thank God and the Catholic communion. I pray that in some small way this project helps aid the cause and good of Christ in the world.

Introduction

IN MANY WAYS, I have been wrestling with this project well before I had ever heard of Scott Hahn. I was raised in southern Georgia in a conservative, evangelical household. We were members of the local Catholic Church, St. Anne's, until when I was around eight years old and my parents came to believe that the Catholic reading of the Bible was insufficient. They had started attending a neighborhood Bible study led by a Southern Baptist family and became convinced that for the good of their family, they needed to find a church that took the Scriptures more seriously than it seemed our priest did. Within a few short years, we had found a small, nondenominational church to call our spiritual home for the remainder of my childhood.

It was not until I reached college that I experienced my crisis of faith. My home church had taught me that the Bible was the perfect Word of God and that in reading it faithfully, the world was completely laid bare. That is, in reading the Scriptures, again, *faithfully*, I would see clearly right from wrong, friend from enemy, and good from evil. In leaving my hometown and attending school in Atlanta, my world became exponentially larger very, very quickly. The assurance that the Bible had given me that I was, in a sense, finished with the work of understanding the world and had firmly moved into the mode of *saving* it, entirely vanished.

Such a development was not just a hiccup in my plan to "seek and save" the world of the lost, it was *devastating*. In losing my confidence in the absolute perfection of the Scriptures, I saw myself as losing my faith. I stopped attending church services with any sort or regularity. I turned to the Scriptures less and less. I distanced myself from other Christians who still demonstrated vibrant lives of faith. Moreover, I was plagued with the fear that I had damned myself, stepped outside of the perfect love of God, and exposed myself to that side of God that looked a lot like vengeful hatred, but I had always been taught could not be. In desperation, I turned to a professor who had become something of a trusted mentor. "I don't understand."

"I don't know how to fix this." "I don't know what to do." And then, finally, "What would you do?" The answer that this kind and patient mentor offered me will stay with me throughout my life.

My professor told me that he understood what I was going through, that there was value in my current suffering, and that the faith out of which I had forced myself may not have been the faith that I thought it was. And then he told me that he would become Catholic. In my religious world, there was no group more confused and tragic than Catholics. Their stained-glass churches, Latin hymns, and bejeweled chalices might have a certain aesthetic appeal, but it certainly was not Christian. My affection for this professor was great enough, however, that I began occasionally to visit a local parish. Over the next several months, I began to discover a faith that, to my mind, looked more like the God I still believed in. My questions, doubts, confusion, and even anger were welcomed.

Thus, during my senior year of college, I asked to begin, along with my older brother and sister-in-law who had been directed to Catholicism by the same professor even if for different reasons, the process of returning to the Catholic faith. And at the Easter Vigil in 2005, I was confirmed in the faith. To my delight, in the old, beautiful parish I had joined, I became confident in my faith, again. Not only did I become more confident in my faith, but I enjoyed my life of faith, particularly going to Mass. Here, finally, I had found a faith in which both my belief and unbelief could rest.

In the years that followed, however, I noticed that there were parts of my newly found Catholicism that began to remind me of the faith of my past. There were those (and sometimes myself) who claimed to have a corner on *authentic* Catholicism. There were those (and again, sometimes myself) who at times imagined their Catholic faith rendered the world utterly knowable, understandable, and straightforward. While I found in the saints numerous moving depictions of long dark nights of the soul, I continued to long for simplicity in the face of so much confusion and certainty in the face of doubt. The more certain and simple the Catholic faith was depicted, however, the less it resembled the complicated and often fractured faith of the ages that I had joined.

Meanwhile, my parents, who had struggled at the time with my conversion, had been given a copy of a book by a Catholic theologian "who actually explained Catholicism in a way that made sense." His name was Scott Hahn. This book, *Rome Sweet Home*, was the recounting of Hahn's own journey to Catholicism, and, as such, my parents found it helpful in understanding their children's decision to convert and eventually led to their own return to Catholicism. While I had never read the book, drowning as I was with the demands of philosophy and then theology graduate work,

Scott Hahn became a name that I heard more than almost any other in my different parish communities over the years as someone uniquely gifted at explaining the faith in an accessible and compelling way.

I wrote a philosophy graduate thesis in which I employed Gottlob Frege's philosophy of language as a response to contemporary defenses of G. E. Moore's Open Question Argument. It was and is by no means perfect, but I was happy with it and, most importantly, I successfully defended it. Several years later, I successfully defended a theology graduate thesis that argued that Bl. John Henry Newman relied on David Hume's theory of knowledge to construct his account of the *illative sense*. There is a lot I would change about it if I could, but I am still proud of the effort and convinced by the argument. When friends and family asked me about them as I was writing them, they did their best to act interested but the conversation would quickly turn to other matters.

When my wife, Beth, and I began dating in 2014, she asked if she could read what I had written and while she made a couple valiant efforts, she never made it all the way through either. She was interested in my ideas and why I felt like they were important, but it was difficult for her to follow all the academic nuances of my theses, given that she did not have the background that I did. I saw value in the work that I had done but my ideas were not connecting with the people in my life I cared about most. In talking with my friends and family, the conversation would often turn to American life and faith.

Despite how much I had come to love the many different theologians whose works now line my bookshelves, they were not the voices that my friends and family were hearing in the Catholic world outside the academy. That voice was Scott Hahn's. My parents had his books and before I met my wife, she and her parents both had his books. Hahn's books were passed out for free at church during Christmas and Easter. He held large youth, adult, and priest conventions, sometimes multiple times a year. Hahn offered marriage retreats and adult education seminars. And despite the fact that Scott Hahn was the loudest voice in shaping the minds of the faithful, as a doctoral student in Catholic theology, I had no idea what he taught. I had never read a single one of his books. I could not tell you how he envisioned Catholic life and faithfulness. Moreover, when I turned to the theological world, I found that no one else had engaged with Hahn either.

The central notion of this project is that, as arguably the most influential voice in American Catholicism, we *should* understand the vision that Scott Hahn offers in his works read by millions of Catholics throughout the world. Hahn is shaping the American Catholic Church in a uniquely powerful manner and yet, until this project, I have been unable to find a single systematic engagement with his thought and work. Thus, this project is an attempt to provide just such an engagement, as well as to bring my own philosophical and theological contributions into the wider world of my loved one's lives of Catholic faithfulness.

To this end, the following project is divided into four chapters. The first chapter, The Life and Thought of Scott Walker Hahn, is a biography of Scott and his wife, Kimberly, his journey of faith, and his work in his St. Paul Center. Most noteworthy of this section is Hahn's education and Catholic conversion at Marquette University. Having provided the details of his conversion and emergence as a Catholic theologian, this is followed by a brief examination of several of his works in order to provide a working understanding of his theological approach and commitments.

The second chapter, Revelation's Gift of the Mass, tracks Hahn's commitments within a fully fleshed theological system in the form of his book, *The Lamb's Supper*. Here, Hahn provides insight into both his exegetical and liturgical frameworks. In this, not only do we get a glimpse of the manner in which Hahn perceives authentic Catholic worship, but also the ways in which he recognizes the Mass and the book of Revelation as lenses through which to view each other.

Hahn's exegetical approach is more deeply explored in chapter 3, Benedict the Inerrantist? There is no single theologian more influential on his work and faith than Pope-Emeritus Benedict XVI. As a self-professed biblical inerrantist, Hahn seeks to demonstrate through his *Covenant and Communion* that inerrantism has always been a part of Catholic tradition and that this is most clear through the exegetical contributions of Benedict. This chapter explores Hahn's understanding of Benedict's biblical commitments and the degree to which Hahn faithfully reproduces his theology.

The final chapter, The Fundamentals of a Truly Catholic America, examines the manner by which Hahn deploys his exegetical and theological commitments in order to present a blueprint for a Catholic reformation of American society and culture. His book, *The First Society*, provides a complete vision of what Hahn recognizes as the ills of western postmodern morality as well as a return to the sacrament of marriage as the key to restoring American society. The chapter concludes with an overview of the philosophical and theological perspectives with which Hahn shares the most in common.

I argue in what follows that the Catholic vision that Hahn *claims* to be providing his audience is, in fact, quite different than the one he *actually presents*. As this vision is delivered to millions of the faithful who look to Hahn as a trustworthy guide to an authentic life of Catholic faith, it is crucial that we offer a critical engagement with his work. It is my hope that this project succeeds at this important task as well as act as a reminder to those of us in the academy that our Catholic friends and loved ones desire accessible theological insight. Moreover, at present, this largely resides in the work of Scott Hahn and his compatriots, whose audience is massive and commitments are not often be representative of the Catholic tradition.

1

The Life and Thought of Scott Walker Hahn

THE HISTORY OF CATHOLIC thought is full of powerful stories of conversion and transformation but none, perhaps, is so well-known as that of St. Augustine of Hippo. Born in northern Africa in AD 354 to a pagan father, Patricius, and a Christian mother, Monica, the young Augustine inhabited two very different worlds. While offered a Christian education and initiation,[1] the young Augustine looked more like his non-believing father than his saintly mother. Despite his Christian formation, Augustine was also greatly influenced by his father, who encouraged him to give himself over to sexual desires and pagan thought. While never completely abandoning his Christian formation, Augustine sank deeply into adolescent sin and pride:

> Around me lay the quagmire of carnal desire, bubbling with the springs of pubescence, and breathing a mist that left my heart fog-bound and benighted; I could no longer tell the clear skies of love from the dark clouds of lust. The two swirled around me in confusion; and in my youthful ignorance I was quickly drawn over the cliffs of desire and sucked down by the eddying currents of vice. . . . I was seething with fornications; overflowing, spilling out, boiling over. O my Joy at last! You said nothing

---

1. Augustine, *The Confessions of Saint Augustine*, 16. Augustine tells us that he while he was not baptized in his youth he was "seasoned with salt," which is a reference to a rite offered to Christian catechumen.

then, as I wandered further and further from you, sowing more and more seeds that would yield no harvest but sorrows.[2]

He finally abandons the path of righteousness at the now infamous pear trees, from which he and his friends stole the fruit only to throw the pears away. This moment stood out for Augustine in that it was the first time that he could remember choosing sin simply for the sake of being sinful. "My evil was loathsome, and I loved it," he confessed, "I was in love with my own ruin and rebellion."[3] Yet, while he had abandoned God, God had not abandoned him, though it would take a long and painful path back for Augustine to see it.

In order to complete his education, Augustine's father sent him off to Carthage to study rhetoric. It was there that he was introduced to Cicero's *Hortensius*, an unfortunately lost dialogue. While inspiring him to devote himself to the study of philosophy, *Hortensius* led Augustine to begin to contrast the Christian Scriptures, particularly the Hebrew Scriptures, with the work of Cicero and the great philosophers of history. Augustine maintains that he always held Christ in high esteem, but "swollen in pride," he found the Scriptures themselves failing to reach the rhetorical heights of Cicero.[4] It was this haughty criticism of the Scriptures that moved Augustine to join the Manichees.[5]

What Augustine found so powerful about Manichaeism was its regard for Christ, something *Hortensius* never offered, while being willing to reject the anthropomorphic depiction of God of the Old Testament. This God, the Manichees contested, was bound by a body, that is, by matter and, thus, appeared to be tossed by the whims of embodied emotion. It was the light, identified by the teachings of Christ that, according to the Manichees, offered a rejection of the flesh, weakness, and superstition. In short, Manichaeism privileged the intellect. While Augustine was still mired in sin, especially sexual sin, Manichaeism taught that if you were intelligent enough, if you were dispassionate enough, if you were high-minded enough, you could

2. Augustine, *The Confessions of Saint Augustine*, 32.
3. Augustine, *The Confessions of Saint Augustine*, 36.
4. Augustine, *The Confessions of Saint Augustine*, 50.
5. Exactly how deeply Augustine immersed himself into a singular body of doctrines actually known as Manichaeism as well as how many of these ideas remained in the Christian Augustine's account of Christian theology is under some question. Given that Augustine names "the Manichees" in his *Confessions*, we will continue under the assumption that he was indeed a Manichee for a time and that his eventual conversion to Christianity brought about a correction or evolution of any lingering Manichean doctrines. For a more complete discussion, see Van den Berg, ed., *In Search of Truth*, particularly Part Three: Studies in Manichaeism and Augustine.

overcome your sinfulness. And that was what Augustine sought and could never accomplish:

> Down one path I pursued the vanity that is popular acclaim; eager for the applause of the theatre, the prizes of poetry, the contests for crowns of grass, the empty show of the public pageants, the intemperance of my lusts. Down the other I sought to be cleansed from those stains . . . .[6]

What Augustine had learned alongside rhetoric and philosophy was exactly how massively intelligent he really was. And yet, all of his years studying the philosophy of the Manichees could not free him from the prison of his sinfulness. Even the many books of the Neoplatonists, by which he hoped to further refine his philosophical acumen, provided no escape from the chains of his sexual immorality.

In his brokenness, however, God sought him. His years of study, while reinforcing certain aspects of his prideful sinfulness, compelled him to search for purer and purer truth. His desire for the knowledge that would allow him to understand his world and free him from his immorality eventually led him back to Christianity. Having moved from Carthage to Milan, Augustine was introduced to the bishop of Milan, Ambrose. It was Ambrose who taught him the allegorical interpretation of the Old Testament.[7] During his time in Milan under the tutelage of Ambrose, Augustine begins to describe himself as, once again, a Christian.

Yet, this is not the moment of his conversion. His philosophical completion under Ambrose, provided in Book Seven, allowed him to recognize the vivacity of Christian thought.[8] It was not, however, until Book Eight that his conversion is made final.[9] Following a conversation with his friends about faith, Augustine found himself alone. Broken and weeping, he walked outside and sat beneath a tree in the garden attached to his home. He finally knew the truth, his friends had helped him find that for which he had spent

---

6. Augustine, *The Confessions of Saint Augustine*, 65.

7. Asiedu, "The Song of Songs and the Ascent of the Soul," 299.

8. The role of Ambrose in Augustine's actual conversion has been questioned, for instance, by Gary Wills who argues in his *Saint Augustine's Conversion* that Ambrose's influence was minimal, as well as in Robert J. O'Connell's *Soundings in St. Augustine's Imagination* who holds that Ambrose could not have been in Milan during Augustine's conversion. These challenges notwithstanding, we will follow the traditional wisdom that Ambrose's tutelage was instrumental in Augustine coming to his Christian faith.

9. The complicated interplay of the intellectual and spiritual or psychological aspects of Augustine's conversion is still widely discussed. To understand these different motivations in his conversion, see: Nauta, "The Prodigal Son"; Dobell, *Augustine's Intellectual Conversion*; O'Connell, S.J., *Images of Conversion in St. Augustine's Confessions*.

his life searching, but he was still not free from the prison of his sin. Hearing a neighboring child at play singing, "Pick it up and read it,"[10] Augustine took it as divine intervention, picked himself up and opened a nearby copy of the book of Romans and read, "Not in riotousness and drunkenness, not in lewdness and wantonness, not in strife and rivalry; but put on the Lord Jesus Christ, and make no provision for the flesh and its lust."[11] Augustine discovered that he could not save himself. He could not simply know enough to free himself from his prison of sin. It was only in setting aside his swollen pride and allowing Christ to be his strength that Augustine finally found freedom.

Augustine found salvation only once he turned away from confidence in his own genius and, in recognition of his weaknesses, relied on the strength and compassion of others.

Scott W. Hahn was born in 1957 as the youngest of three children to Fred and Molly Lou Hahn. Born and raised just outside of Pittsburgh, Pennsylvania, Hahn describes his family as the most nominal of Christians for whom church attendance was rare and predominantly socially motivated.[12] Baptized as a Presbyterian, the young Hahn had almost no religious interest until, following a period of teenage rebellion that very nearly landed him in a juvenile detention center, a friend convinced him to attend with him a meeting of the evangelical organization known as Young Life.[13] While initially only convinced to go so as to spend more time with a romantic interest, it was through Young Life that he met one of the leaders who eventually led him to Christianity. "Early in my high school years I made a commitment and asked Jesus Christ into my heart," he writes, "I asked him to be my savior and Lord."[14]

Hahn took to his new Christian faith with the same energy he had previously applied to teenage angst and rebellion and committed himself to studying the Bible, under the guidance of his Young Life friends, as much as possible. He recounts that by the time he graduated from high school, he had read the entirety of the Scriptures "two or three times"[15] and had fallen "head over heels in love with the Word of God—the inerrant, infallible guide to our life as Christians—and with the study of theology."[16] Over these years,

10. Augustine, *Confessions of Saint Augustine*, 182.
11. Augustine, *Confessions of Saint Augustine*, 183
12. Hahn, *Rome Sweet Home*, 1.
13. Hahn, *Rome Sweet Home*, 2.
14. Hahn, "The Scott Hahn Conversion Story."
15. Hahn, "The Scott Hahn Conversion Story."
16. Hahn, *Rome Sweet Home*, 5.

his Young Life leader taught him to not just read the Bible, but to "soak in it to read it and re-read it from beginning to end."[17] This dramatic shift resulted in the newly passionate Hahn manifesting a deeply anti-Catholic bias. The high school Hahn attacked Catholic belief and encouraged Catholic friends to leave the Church for the sake of their souls. In a particularly poignant passage, Hahn even describes taking the rosary of his newly deceased lifelong Catholic grandmother and ripping it to pieces while praying the she would now be free of the chains of Catholic belief that had bound her in life.[18]

Naturally, this intensely energetic Christian conversion brought Hahn to attend a Christian college following high school in order to pursue a career in ministry. Majoring in philosophy, theology in Scripture, and economics, Hahn devoted much of his energy while at Grove City College, academically and personally, to Christian evangelization and apologetics. Specifically targeting Catholic doctrine and Catholic young people who seemingly had no working understanding of Catholic doctrine, Hahn saw himself as singularly focused on inspiring devotion to the Scriptures and fundamentals of the faith to the unchurched and non-Protestant. It was during his studies at Grove City that he met Kimberly, and he describes their evolving relationship largely in terms of their mutually growing commitment to proselytization and apologetics.

Having completed their undergraduate degrees, Scott and Kimberly got married and moved to Massachusetts to pursue graduate degrees at Gordon-Conwell Theological Seminary. After three years, Hahn graduated at the top of his class, which he mentions only "to illustrate how [he] pursued [his] studies with a sort of vengeance."[19] As he describes it, the passion and rigor with which he and Kimberly approached their graduate studies refused easy answers or overly simplistic justification. Hahn recounts a particular period late in his undergraduate formation in which many of his friends who had been christened as infants began to become interested in getting rebaptized. While his companions all parroted the standard presentation of believer's baptism, Hahn confesses that while uncertain about the issue, he at least knew the answer "wasn't to play 'follow the leader.'"[20] The following week, his friends all got rebaptized while he dedicated himself to studying the issue more, even agreeing to write a paper for a class he was taking at the time on the question of infant baptism.

17. Hahn, "The Scott Hahn Conversion Story."
18. Hahn, "The Scott Hahn Conversion Story."
19. Hahn, "The Scott Hahn Conversion Story."
20. Hahn, *Rome Sweet Home*, 15.

Kimberly had a similar event take place at Gordon-Conwell. During a Christian Ethics course, she was given a group project assignment concerning contraception. The self-proclaimed member of the group announced that the conclusion was already manifest that contraception (excluding, of course, abortifacients) was entirely permissible and that the only Christians who had ever thought differently were the Catholics. "Well, that kind of argumentation didn't really impress Kimberly," Hahn writes, "and she took an interest in researching this on her own."[21] In both cases, they discovered that their suspicions were right and that the remainder of their Christian cohorts were surprisingly uninformed about what the Scriptures actually taught.

This period of graduate studies, of questioning the simple assumptions of his colleagues, brought Hahn to an obsession with the Hebrew notion of covenant. As he began examining the Scriptures, particularly in light of his burgeoning proficiency in Hebrew and Greek, Hahn became increasingly convinced that the unifying element of the Scriptures was this idea.[22] A defining moment for Hahn's wrestling with the meaning of covenant came while attending a Sunday morning church service where one of his Gordon-Conwell professors was the pastor. As with the majority of evangelical services, the emphasis of the service was on the sermon, the topic of which, as it was just a week before Easter, was the Passion. As the sermon drew towards a close, something unexpected happened. The pastor recounted the words of Jesus on the cross, "It is finished," and then stopped and asked the congregation if they had ever wondered exactly *what*, for Jesus, had been finished.[23] This Harvard trained Hebrew professor who later went on to receive his doctorate from Oxford University confessed that he did not actually know the answer. Such an admission shocked Hahn and, following the conclusion of the service, he challenged the pastor who merely repeated his earlier claim. Then he said something to Hahn that, unknowingly, would define the rest of his career and life. "He repeated his assurance that he couldn't answer it," Hahn tells us, "but then he assured me that I would."[24] Hahn took these words to heart. His Harvard trained pastor could not answer this question but Hahn, for some reason that both the pastor and Hahn himself recognized but could not explain, would be the one who would.

Hahn devoted the remainder of his research to discovering the referent for that simple pronoun, "it," and his study eventually led him to an analysis of the Hebrew celebration of Passover. Given his reformed context,

21. Hahn, "The Scott Hahn Conversion Story."
22. Hahn, *Rome Sweet Home*, 29.
23. Hahn, *The Fourth Cup*, 20.
24. Hahn, *The Fourth Cup*, 21.

Hahn turned to Calvin's engagement with Passover and his insistence that the celebration was so important to Israel because it was in that feast every year that they renewed their covenant with God. Calvin seemed to be in agreement with Hahn's own conviction that the notion of covenant functioned as an exegetical key to the Scriptures, yet in Calvin's explication of covenant, the Passover was a renewal of something akin to a legal contract between God and Israel.[25] The more he studied, however, the more he became convinced that the Hebrew notions of covenant and contract were entirely distinct. For the ancient Hebrews, he discovered, in a contract one exchanges property while in a covenant one exchanges persons.[26] That is, covenants in the Hebrew Scriptures *created sacred family bonds*. Thus, when Jesus instituted the new covenant in his blood at the Last Supper, itself a seder of Passover, he was not simply creating a contractual arrangement in which we exchange our sin for his righteousness, but more importantly creating a sacred familial kinship into which we are all invited.[27]

It was in this discussion that Hahn began to question the hallowed *sola fide* of Calvinist theology. In his intense study of the Scriptures, it became clear to him that the New Testament writers understood faith itself to be insufficient for salvation, in that the act of participation in the sacrifice of

    25. Hahn, *The Fourth Cup*, 23.
    26. Hahn, "The Scott Hahn Conversion Story."
    27. Hahn, *Rome Sweet Home*, 30. It should be noted that here Hahn provides us with a critical insight into his thought. In reference to Luther's and Calvin's legal explication of redemption, Hahn remarks, "Although true, that explanation fell short of the full truth of the Gospel." Hahn writes this in his now Catholic state, but it is not at all clear that the Church would accept Luther's and Calvin's examinations of redemption as even *partially* true. First and foremost, there is the historical-critical question as to whether or not a sixteenth-century legal explication of Christ's redemptive act would in any way correlate to the legal language employed in the New Testament. In the Greco-Roman world, the family unit demonstrated a certain legal precedent in that the *pater familia* was often depicted as enjoying a definitive, unquestionable authority over the members of his family. According to Jewish law, a father had an obligation to carry out justice within the family unit. Moreover, the absolute authority of the monarch was often justified in reference to the place of a patriarch within his family. In turn, the authority of a father was explained in terms of the likeness of a ruler to their subjects. It is an important question as to whether or not the legal characterization of redemption Luther and Calvin offer is not more akin to the familial relationship in the ancient Greco-Roman world than its legal system. For further discussion of the analogical relationship between legal and familial authority, see Favro, "Pater urbis"; Saller, "Pater Familias, Mater Familias, and the Gendered Semantics of the Roman Household"; Michael Joseph Brown, "Paul's Use of ΔΟΥΛΟΣ ΧΡΙΣΤΟΥ ΙΗΣΟΥ in Romans 1:1." Secondly, it is not at all clear that the Church today would accept this depiction involving debts and obligation, as such a presentation entirely excludes the kenotic dimension of Christ's salvific act. Given these difficulties with Hahn's claim, it is an open question as to the purchase even his qualified sanction of reformation soteriology provides.

the Eucharist was understood as establishing, both for those who offer it as well as those who receive it, a new family bond established in the covenant.[28] That is, belief is recognized as being necessary for covenant, but without being coupled with participation in the sacrifice of the Eucharist, belief is in itself insufficient. Such a realization naturally created much discomfort for the deeply anti-Catholic Hahn, as it threatened the very foundation of his Reformed commitments. Yet, this study was opening his eyes to the truly radical nature of New Testament Christianity. "In the first and second century," Hahn contends, "the most striking thing about Christianity was probably how little it looked like a *religion*."[29] The absence of blood sacrifice in the Christian faith was because in offering himself Christ had completed, or finished, the Passover hope of God's covenant with Israel. Hahn realized, however, that we needed both. That is, we need the redemption accomplished at the resurrection as well as the completion of the covenant made at the crucifixion. For Hahn, we have faith in the redemptive work of Christ but we participate in his covenantal sacrifice. What remained unclear for Hahn at this time was exactly how we participate.

Having finished their graduate studies at Gordon-Conwell, the Hahns moved to Fairfax, Virginia for Scott to take a position as pastor of Trinity Presbyterian Church. Through his preaching and teaching there, Hahn began teaching what he had discovered during his studies at Gordon-Conwell. Namely, that the covenant is central and is bound to the crucifixion

---

28. Hahn, *The Fourth Cup*, 44.

29. Hahn, *The Fourth Cup*, 41. It should be noted that this statement seems to be somewhat in tension with his claims elsewhere concerning the liturgies of the New Testament and early Church. For instance, in his *Consuming the Word* (p. 47), he remarks, "Recent research has made academic readers more sensitive to liturgical forms embedded in the Epistles. To first-century authors and their audiences, such forms would have been incomprehensible apart from some sense of sacrifice." He continues on in the above discussion to claim that the reason first- and second-century observers would not have easily recognized Christianity as a religion was because of the lack of a blood sacrifice, which was present in every other ancient near-eastern religious practice. First and foremost, it is not at all clear that blood sacrifice was a prominent feature of every ancient religion. The Roman Imperial mystery cults, for instance, were varied, complicated, and appeared to resist any sort of unifying codification. If we also look at Greek paganism in Plato, one of the only references to sacrifice appears to be during Socrates' execution in the *Phaedo* in which, as his famous last words, he reminds his followers that he owes a sacrifice to Asclepius. Despite his many discussions of religion and belief, Socrates never identifies the practice of faith with sacrifice. Second, if we look at Justin Martyr's *First Apology*, we find Martyr defending the early Christians from the widely held criticism that in their ceremonies the Christians were practicing cannibalism. Moreover, the language that the early Christian martyrs reserved for themselves was often as offering themselves as a kind of sacrificial rite for the aid of the Church in the world.

of Christ; Christ makes this connection clear at the Last Supper, and there instituted as a practice in which Christians are to take part. Given the centrality of the Eucharist in Hahn's understanding of the faith at this point, he moved his congregations toward weekly celebrations of Communion rather than simply quarterly. With this change, Hahn began to catalog all of the developments to his theology and faith practice over a relatively short period of time. It was at this moment that Hahn realized, with what he describes as horror, what was actually taking place. "All of a sudden," Hahn confesses, "the Roman Catholic Church that I opposed seemed to be coming up with the right answer on one thing after another, much to my shock and dismay."[30]

It was during this same time period that Hahn also took up teaching Scripture at a private Christian high school in the area. After a discussion about the development of the covenant from a small Old Testament tribe to a worldwide family of faith, one of his students confessed that the remainder of his students had discussed it privately and decided that Hahn was on the cusp of conversion to Catholicism. In horror, he went home that day and shared the encounter with Kimberly. Expecting her to share in his outrage, she simply responded, "Well, are you?"[31] Feeling betrayed, Hahn stormed away and returned to his studies. A little later, Hahn took a position at a local Presbyterian seminary and was teaching his students about the Gospel of John. Upon reaching the Bread of Life passage from John 6, he grew uncomfortable in the recognition that, if he was being honest with himself, Jesus never softens the language of eating his flesh and drinking his blood. In fact, when the people were troubled by the graphic nature of his teaching, Jesus turned to his disciples and asked them if they would leave him, too. Soon after this discussion, a student asked in class for Hahn to explain where the cherished Reformation mantra *sola scriptura* was itself found in the Scriptures. He, again, had no response.

Hahn recalls driving home in a panic and began reaching out to other theologians. In reaching out to a particular "Oxford trained" theologian, he was told that Christians have no option but simply to maintain the assumption of *Scripture only* even while recognizing that the assumption is itself not founded in Scripture.[32] At every turn, his Reformed commitments

---

30. Hahn, *Rome Sweet Home*, 46.

31. Hahn, "The Scott Hahn Conversion Story."

32. Hahn, "The Scott Hahn Conversion Story." It should be mentioned that there are many defenses of the Protestant doctrine of *sola scriptura* of which an "Oxford trained" theologian should have been aware. For current examples, see Burger, Huijgen, and Peels, eds., *Sola Scriptura*; and Peckham, "*Sola Scriptura: Reductio Ad Absurdum*," Wiley "Tradition and Sola Scriptura in 2 Thessalonians 2:15."

were being eroded and his attempts to bolster his defenses by reaching out to those around him were turning up empty. One of those that he reached out to eventually responded by asking Hahn if he was actually planning on becoming Catholic, to which he could only respond, "I hope not."[33] Unsure as he was about the future, however, Hahn knew that his answer must be "no" when the seminary at which he was working came and offered him a permanent position as dean of the seminary. When Kimberly asked him why he could not accept the position he responded that, with his theological commitments in chaos, he did not know what he could actually teach. Such a realization, he saw, also meant that he needed to resign as pastor of his church. Thus, the Hahns packed up their young family and moved back to Pennsylvania where Hahn took a job as an administrative assistant to the president of his *alma mater*, Grove City College.

During his time as an assistant to the president of Grove City College, Hahn threw himself into researching the questions that had been causing him so much anxiety. On a trip to his in-laws in Cincinnati, Hahn came across a used bookstore that had just received the entire library of a well-known priest and Scripture scholar who had recently passed away. Over the next several years, Hahn thinks he must have read around two hundred of the books from the late priest's library. It was through this that he was able to discover the truth of Catholic doctrine. Hahn confessed to Kimberly one evening that he felt that God might be calling him into the Catholic faith.[34] More than any other aspect of his study, it was his engagement with the Church Fathers, particularly in their engagement with the Gospel of John, that opened him to the possibility that the Catholic perspective on the Scriptures was correct.

Yet, while his own study was confirming Catholic doctrine more and more, his experience with Catholics themselves just added more confusion. Despite Kimberly's wishes, he sought out Catholic priests to discuss the Church with him. Hahn claims he was told by several priests that Vatican II had concluded that it was not necessary for one to convert to the Catholic faith and that the best thing for him would be to remain in his current community and "to be the best Presbyterian you can be."[35] Hahn had also started attending some theology courses at Duquesne University where he found himself "the only student defending Pope John Paul II" and "explaining to priests (and even ex-priests) how certain Catholic beliefs were

---

33. Hahn, *Rome Sweet Home*, 54.
34. Hahn, *Rome Sweet Home*, 60.
35. Hahn, *Rome Sweet Home*, 66.

grounded in Scripture."[36] Even as he was becoming increasingly convinced that the Church held the answers for which he had been looking, he had also become ever more convinced that almost no one, Protestant or Catholic, knew or believed what the Catholic Church actually teaches.

During this time, however, Hahn and a friend, Gerry, whom he had pulled into his investigation of Catholicism, continued to read and research for themselves, all the while with Kimberly praying earnestly that she could find Catholicism's fatal flaw. One notable attempt at resisting the call of the Catholic faith involved a discussion with a former professor. John Gerstner, whom Hahn describes as "a Harvard-trained, Calvinist theologian with strong anti-Catholic convictions," was eager to sit down with Hahn and Gerry in order to save them from the errors of Catholicism. Gerstner, however, turned out not to be the interlocutor for which they had been hoping. Hahn recalls that at one point in the conversation, Gerstner asked him to provide scriptural support for the pope. Hahn replied by referencing Peter's receiving the keys of the kingdom from Matthew 16:17–19. He went on to explain that the notion of the keys of the kingdom has an Old Testament analog in the book of Isaiah where the king, Hezekiah, denotes a new leader in his court by giving him "keys to the kingdom." The "Harvard-trained" Gerstner responds, "That's a clever argument, Scott." When asked how Protestants can refute it, Gerstner confesses, "Well, I'm not sure I've ever heard it before."[37] Hours of conversation ensued on a host of other topics, but at no point did Gerstner provide Hahn and Gerry with anything approaching a sufficient defense of his anti-Catholic position. Instead, he appeared to punt on every point, yet continued to stubbornly cling to his position. Upon returning home and relaying the conversation to Kimberly, she asked him to not convert abruptly as it would be too painful. Hahn in turn promised that if he came to believe it necessary, he would at least not convert before 1990. As it was currently 1985, he felt that would be a reasonable amount of time to decide the right path for himself, and for Kimberly to join him

---

36. Hahn, *Rome Sweet Home*, 66.

37. Hahn, *Rome Sweet Home*, 71. Here again, Hahn describes an authority on Protestant theology by citing their pedigree (i.e., "Oxford-trained," "Harvard-trained," etc.) only to go on to describe them as unaware of significant defenses of Protestant positions. The recognition of the complex character of the "keys of the kingdom" imagery in Old Testament tradition is widely recognized within both Catholic and Protestant literature. See, Kingsbury, "The Figure of Peter in Matthew's Gospel as a Theological Problem"; Dahlberg, "The Typological Use of Jeremiah 1:4–19 in Matthew 16:13–23"; Barber, "Jesus as the Davidic Temple Builder and Peter's Priestly Role in Matthew 16:16–19." Interestingly, Michael Barber is a member of Hahn's St. Paul Center and, yet, his article maintains that the connection between Matthew 16:19 and Isaiah 22:22 has been well-established.

on the journey.³⁸ While he was not yet ready to enter the Catholic faith, Hahn decided he needed to study along with Catholics full-time and, thus, applied and was accepted into the theology doctoral program at Marquette University.³⁹

It was as a first-year doctoral student at Marquette that Hahn actually attended his first Catholic Mass.

> With my Bible and a notebook, I took a seat in the back pew at the university chapel. I was well prepared. I had taken every precaution. I could not have been safer if I'd been locked in a plastic observation bubble. But I soon found that I wasn't prepared at all. What I was experiencing was an immersion in Scripture—both the Old Testament and the New. But it wasn't at all like a Bible study. It wasn't at all like class. There was nothing about it that anyone would find entertaining. There was nothing that seemed calculated or calibrated to stir my emotions. The words and the worship were directed toward God. They were about God. . . .The rite of the Mass was evoking heaven—as if we were really there . . . .⁴⁰

This experience confirmed spiritually what he was intellectually finding as he "sat and filled notebooks in Marquette's theological library."⁴¹ Sitting by himself in the back of Mass as an outsider, Hahn confesses that he was "salivating—and weeping" for the Eucharist, which he finally realized was really Jesus.⁴² "Lord, I want you. I want communion more fully with you," Hahn prayed there in the pew, "You've come into my heart. You're my personal Savior and Lord, but now I think You want to come onto my tongue and into my stomach, and into my body as well as my soul until this communion is complete."⁴³

Hahn returned home incredibly conflicted. The truth of the Mass had finally been fully revealed to him, but he was bound by the promise he made to his wife. He had begun attending Mass daily and had only become increasingly more convinced that the Catholic Church was the Church

---

38. Hahn, *Rome Sweet Home*, 76.
39. Hahn, *The Fourth Cup*, 142.
40. Hahn, *The Fourth Cup*, 145.
41. Hahn, *The Fourth Cup*, 155. The fact that Hahn describes his intellectual conversion as taking place alone in "Marquette's theological library" rather than through engagement with Marquette's theological community is an important insight into the manner by which Hahn understands himself and the state of Catholic academia. This will be discussed more fully in later sections.
42. Hahn, *The Fourth Cup*, 155.
43. Hahn, "The Scott Hahn Conversion Story."

initiated by Christ in Peter still present in the world today. Two weeks before Easter in 1986, Hahn received a shocking call from his friend Gerry, who let him know that both he and his wife would be joining the Church at the Easter Vigil. After talking with Gerry, he went downstairs and asked Kimberly to release him from his promise. "Kimberly I don't know how to say this," Hahn confessed, "but I'm afraid I've reached the point where to delay obedience would be disobedience."[44] After a period of prayer, Kimberly released her husband from his promise, but also explaining to him that she felt betrayed and abandoned by her husband.

His decision having been made, and Kimberly freeing him to follow his conscience, Hahn went to a nearby parish where he told the pastor about his plans to join the Church. The pastor understanding his conviction and plight, agreed to aid Hahn in his conversion. And thus, two weeks later, at the Easter Vigil in 1986, with his family and grieving wife sitting with him, Hahn was given conditional baptism, reconciliation, confirmation, and First Communion. He was finally a member of the Roman Catholic Church. And Kimberly still was not. When he returned to the pew, he put his arm around her and could feel the Eucharist in him reaching out to her.[45] Kimberly, on the other hand, described it as the worst night of her life.[46]

The next few years were both periods of great growth as well as deep pain. The Hahn's marriage struggled under the pain of spiritual estrangement, yet Hahn was gaining a deeper understanding of the faith. As he had built a career as an evangelical pastor and teacher, however, he soon found himself without a steady income. Through the recommendation of a member of the Marquette theology department, Hahn received an offer to teach philosophy from the College of St. Francis in Joliet, Illinois. He accepted the position and the Hahns moved soon after the birth of their third child. During his short time in Joliet, Hahn began to connect with prominent Catholic contributors and organizations. He gave lectures and interviews for Catholic Answers (a Catholic apologetics-based ministry), St. Joseph Communications (the company through which Hahn would go on to sell many of his books and Catholic media offerings), and even EWTN's Mother Angelica. All of this eventually led to a call from the chair of the theology department at Franciscan University of Steubenville, informing Hahn of an opening in the department the following year. Following several interviews, he was informed that he had been offered the position. In 1990, then, Hahn moved his family out to Steubenville, Ohio and, quite

---

44. Hahn, *Rome Sweet Home*, 90.
45. Hahn, *Rome Sweet Home*, 92.
46. Hahn, *Rome Sweet Home*, 95.

unexpectedly to Hahn, Kimberly decided to enter the Church at the Easter Vigil.[47] It turns out that in Kimberly's frantic search for Catholicism's fatal flaw she found none; instead, she heard the voice of God calling her home to the Church of the Apostles.

It was his position at Franciscan that provided the grounds for Hahn to establish his incredible reach. While Hahn did not receive his doctorate from Marquette until 1995, he and Kimberly published their *Rome Sweet Home* to much acclaim in 1993 and it has gone on to sell hundreds of thousands of copies. A recording of his conversion story, which Hahn refers to simply as "The Tape," had sold hundreds of thousands of copies by the time *Rome Sweet Home* was published. He has gone on to publish nearly sixty books, twenty academic articles, and countless popular level articles. In 2001, Hahn founded the St. Paul Center for Biblical Theology.

The St. Paul Center, which describes itself as a "non-profit research and educational institute that promotes life-transforming Scripture study in the Catholic tradition," has been the vehicle through which Hahn has had the greatest effect on the Catholic Church, particularly in the United States.[48] The Center boasts almost seventy fellows, all of whom have either doctoral degrees, are Catholic priests, or both. Included in this list are prominent Catholic voices such as Robert Louis Wilken, Archbishop Terrence Pendergast, Fr. Jeremy Driscoll, Matthew Levering (himself author or editor of over thirty academic books), and Bishop Robert Barron.[49] It is also home to Emmaus Road Publishing, which currently offers 362 books, and the journals *Nova et Vetera* and *Letter & Spirit*, an academic journal created by the Center, numerous audio and video offerings, free online spiritual and theological courses, a podcast, and a radio station.[50] Lastly, every year the Center offers conferences for priests as well as events for the laity, pilgrimages to both the Holy Land and Italy, and numerous speaking engagements for both Scott and Kimberly. From June 2019 to the beginning of June 2020, his schedule lists over thirty speaking engagements, a number that without doubt would have grown significantly if not for the coronavirus pandemic of 2020.[51]

During this same period, a host of videos of Hahn's speeches or television show appearances have been posted to the website youtube.com and, to date, have over three hundred thousand views. His total views on YouTube number well over three million. At the end of April 2019, Hahn also

---

47. Hahn, *Rome Sweet Home*, 133.
48. "About the Center," St. Paul Center.
49. "Fellows," St. Paul Center.
50. https://stpaulcenter.com/.
51. http://www.scotthahn.com/schedule.

launched a podcast, "The Road to Emmaus with Scott Hahn," which offers over sixty episodes and already has thousands of listeners. The St. Paul Center website, over a six month period in 2020 had roughly 270,000 unique visitors and has over 1.4 million followers on Facebook. Hahn himself has over six hundred thousand followers on the popular social networking site.

As pertains more to the present discussion, one of Hahn's newest books, *Hope to Die: The Christian Meaning of Death and the Resurrection of the Body* (2020), written with Emily Stimpson Chapman, sits at number 5,079 in total book rankings on Amazon.com. That number is set against *every* book sold on Amazon, not just other books in the subject of Catholic Theology or other smaller subsections. In fact, Hahn has three books that ranked within the top twenty thousand and several others within the top fifty thousand. His 2019, *The Lamb's Supper*, is currently ranked number three of all books in the category of Roman Catholicism.

Moreover, Hahn's publishers list options for bulk purchases of both his *Signs of Life* and *Joy to the World*. These listings each include references to special parish pricing with opportunities for the books to be handed out as evangelization tools during Lent and Advent respectively. Such a push to get Hahn' work in the hands of as many people as possible was also offered in 2013 in which Lighthouse Media Company, Ignatius Press, and Hahn announced a joint promotion in which *Rome Sweet Home*, again, the story of the Hahn's conversion, was on sale to parishes across the country for $1 apiece to parishes in the hopes of reaching "1-million Catholics at Christmas." Their lofty aim was for virtually every single Catholic to leave a Christmas service with a copy provided to them by the parish and other supporters for free.[52] In fact, as those close to me became aware that I was writing about Hahn, I was contacted several times by friends in different parts of the country who had been given free copies of his books while leaving Sunday Masses.

And finally, Hahn and the St. Paul Center offer (for purchase) resources for Catholic education, most of which feature Hahn, covering the Bible, the Church Fathers, the biblical account of creation to the coming of Christ, the Virgin Mary, and the Eucharist. Their Didache catechetical series, which includes four textbooks written by Hahn (the only textbooks for which an author is cited in the series), have been translated into complete educational systems and are currently being used in over six hundred Catholic schools across the country.[53] This is not to mention the many conferences,

---

52. https://brandonvogt.com/buck-a-book/.
53. https://www.mycatholicfaithdelivered.com/home.aspx?pagename=Didache.

educational resources, and books offered by the remainder of the members of the St. Paul Society.

In short, Hahn's conversion sitting alone in the back of Mass in 1986 has grown into the single most influential Catholic organization in the United States today. Moreover, the above list fails to include the countless students who have sat in his courses over the past twenty-three years of collegiate teaching. What remains to be seen, however, is the theological vision Hahn is offering throughout these many avenues.

In beginning to analyze Hahn's work, we first need to look for themes and approaches that run through his body of work. Given the incredible breadth of Hahn's corpus, however, this survey chapter focuses on four prominent works that span much of his prolific career. The first, *Hail Holy Queen: The Mother of God in the Word of God*, from 2001, demonstrates Mary's centrality, not just in Catholic theology but in Old Testament prophecy and in the story of salvation. *Reasons to Believe: How to Understand, Explain, and Defend the Catholic Faith*, published in 2007, takes up the notion of Catholic apologetics. *Consuming the Word: The New Testament and the Eucharist in the Early Church*, from 2013, examines the Eucharistic centeredness of the New Testament Church and writings. And finally, *The Creed: Professing the Faith through the Ages* was published in 2016.

In beginning to analyze Hahn's work, it must be noted that much of that work has been written as "Professor of Biblical Theology and the New Evangelization" at Franciscan. That is, Hahn understands himself, first and foremost, as a biblical theologian, and for his vast audience, such a designation will come as no surprise. Hahn employs an impressive amount of Scripture in every book or article he writes, and while he does not hold to the *sola scriptura* (Scripture only) of his evangelical past, it is very clear that he believes it critical that Catholics be able to provide a scriptural foundation for every aspect of the faith. This is nowhere more clear than in his discussions of the Eucharist.

As noted above, Hahn attributes at least the catalyst of his conversion to his encounter of the Eucharist in a Mass he attended as an outsider. Even during his most anti-Catholic moments, the Eucharist was always central to his faith, and alone in the pew at the back of that small chapel in Milwaukee, it was important to Hahn that he be able to follow the Eucharistic sacrifice of the Mass to its scriptural roots.[54] Each book receives a piece of that discussion, but throughout his career, Hahn has devoted a few books entirely to the Eucharist and its scriptural and sacramental relationship to the Church.

---

54. Hahn, *Rome Sweet Home*, 87.

While the identification of the Eucharist as scripturally instituted is most clearly recognized in the recitation of Luke 22:17–20 in Mass, the Scripture passage concerning the Eucharist with which Hahn spends the most time is 1 Corinthians 11:23–25:

> For I received from the Lord what I also delivered to you, that the Lord Jesus, on the night when He was betrayed took bread, and when He had given thanks, broke it, and said, "This is My body which is for you. Do this in remembrance of Me." In the same way also the cup, after supper, saying, "This cup is the new covenant in My blood. Do this as often as you drink it, in remembrance of Me."[55]

Of primary interest to Hahn, is that Paul makes it clear that the institution of the Eucharist at the Last Supper, at which, of course, Paul himself was not present, was recognized by the New Testament leadership as a practice to be replicated in Christian worship. "A command cannot get much simpler or more direct than that: Just do it," Hahn concludes in *Reasons to Believe*, "and so the early Christians *did*, wherever they went."[56] This passage also appears in *Consuming the Word* where Hahn argues it serves a similar purpose. For Hahn, these verses from 1 Corinthians "clearly mark the ritual event that inaugurated the 'New Testament.'"[57] And lastly, these verses also appear in his *The Fourth Cup*, his spiritual autobiography that we relied upon in the discussion above, in which Hahn concludes, "In defining the contents of the cup, Jesus is clearly echoing the words spoken by Moses in the Sinai desert."[58]

In each of the three very different contexts in which Hahn cites 1 Corinthians 11:23–25, he puts the passage to a similar use. Whether he is discussing the nature of the New Testament itself, the story of his own theological walk of faith, or the practice of arguing the defense of the faith, Hahn employs the notion of simplicity or clarity. This idea that the Scriptures speak, for the most part, clearly or simply is a critical feature of Hahn's exegetical vision. He invokes clarity in relation to massively important Christian doctrines, oftentimes despite widespread disagreement in the remainder of the non-Catholic Christian world. In his *The Creed*, Hahn concludes that "the Christian confession was an oath is clear from Philippians 2."[59] The clarity of the Scriptures is crucial for Hahn, particularly in

---

55. 1 Corinthians 11:23–25. Hahn, *Reasons to Believe*, 116.
56. Hahn, *Reasons to Believe*, 116.
57. Hahn, *Consuming the Word*, 21.
58. Hahn, *The Fourth Cup*, 54.
59. Hahn, *The Creed*, 23.

regards to the Eucharist, because it allows each and every Catholic to make the faith their own. "[The] mysteries are unfathomable—inexhaustible—but they are eminently knowable," Hahn exhorts in *Reasons to Believe*, "because *God himself has willed them to be known*."[60] That is, Hahn believes that each of us has an obligation to be prepared to provide an answer to any question asked of us concerning our faith.[61] And with the Eucharist residing at the heart of Catholic worship and faithfulness, "Jesus left no loophole, Hahn concludes."[62] The Bread of Life passage from John 6 and its corresponding initiation into ritual in 1 Corinthians render the Catholic position of transubstantiation, not just inescapable, but easily accessible for every Catholic. For Hahn, more than anything else, the liturgy of the celebration of the Eucharist, that is, the Mass, directs us toward the Scriptures, and the Scriptures allow us, individually, to make sense of the Mass and the mysteries of both Mass and Scripture.[63] The Scriptures are, then, a key that unlocks the secrets of the Catholic faith given to each of us individually, which, again, mirrors his own story of conversion.[64]

In examining Hahn's position regarding the Scriptures, there are, however, a couple of concerns that will need to be addressed as this work moves forward. First, it is not at all clear, according to the tradition, that the Scriptures and the mysteries they invoke should be regarded as so easily accessible by every Christian. Indeed, according to the Second Vatican Council's *Dei Verbum*:

> Sacred theology rests on the written word of God, *together with sacred tradition*, as its primary and perpetual foundation. By scrutinizing the light of faith all truth stored up in the mystery of Christ, theology is most powerfully strengthened and constantly rejuvenated by that word. . . . Therefore, all the clergy must hold fast to the Sacred Scriptures through diligent sacred reading and careful study, especially the priests of Christ and others, such as deacons and catechists who are legitimately active in the mystery of the word . . . *since they must share the abundant wealth of the divine word the faithful committed to them*. . . . It devolves on sacred bishops "who have the apostolic

---

60. Hahn, *Reasons to Believe*, 10.

61. Hahn, *Reason to Believe*, 9. Hahn likens our individual obligation to be fully prepared to explain the faith to the Boy Scouts' well known, "Always be prepared."

62. Hahn, *Reasons to Believe*, 118.

63. Hahn, *Letter and Spirit*, 46.

64. Hahn, *The Lamb's Supper*, 128.

teaching" to give the faithful entrusted to them suitable instruction in the right use of the divine books.[65]

Naturally, *Dei Verbum* instructs the faithful to become familiar with the Scriptures as "ignorance of the Scriptures is ignorance of Christ,"[66] yet it is clear that the individual's relationship to the Scriptures is in familiarity guided towards mystery by those charged with being experts of the faith, the clergy and theologians. Hahn recognizes the need for the Church to guide the faithful in their understanding of the Scriptures, yet appears to envision such guidance as a kind of initiation that comes to completion after which these mysteries can be actualized in a life of faith.[67]

Second, *Dei Verbum* also makes clear that while 2 Timothy absolutely teaches that all Scripture must be viewed as useful for teaching, the Scriptures cannot be regarded as simple:

> However, since God speaks in Sacred Scripture through men in human fashion, the interpreter of Sacred Scripture, in order to see clearly what God wanted to communicate to us, *should carefully investigate what meaning the sacred writers really intended, and what God wanted to manifest by means of their words*. To search out the intention of the sacred writers, *attention should be given, among other things, to "literary forms." For truth is set forth and expressed differently in texts which are variously historical, prophetic, poetic, or of other forms of discourse*. The interpreter must *investigate what meaning the sacred writer intended to express and actually expressed in particular circumstances by using contemporary literary forms in accordance with the situation of his own time and culture*.[68]

It would be difficult to expect each individual Catholic to be prepared to offer such a careful investigation of the different literary forms employed, cultural influences manifest, etc., in the Scriptures so as to easily move from familiarity to "eminent knowability."

This leads us, however, to a second critical feature of Hahn's Catholic vision: *liturgy*. Hahn makes clear that liturgy is first and foremost Scripture. "All of Scripture is intrinsically liturgical," Hahn claims at the outset of *Letter and Spirit*, "Liturgy is like a golden thread that runs through the many pearls of salvation history and holds them together."[69] Indeed, Hahn

---

65. Paul VI, *Dei Verbum*, §25–26, emphasis added.
66. Paul VI, *Dei Verbum*, §25.
67. Hahn, *Consuming the Word*, 114.
68. Paul VI, *Dei Verbum*, §12, emphasis added.
69. Hahn, *Letter and Spirit*, 35.

goes on to demonstrate that in Creation God "made time holy, and creation itself becomes a cosmic temple with Adam as its high priest."[70] This liturgical exegetical key remains in place for Hahn throughout the entirety of the Scriptures. It continues through the Pentateuch,[71] the prophets,[72] Wisdom literature,[73] the Gospels,[74] the Pauline letters,[75] and Revelation.[76] This is only to be expected, Hahn tells us, as "liturgy and Scripture possess a formal unity."[77] That is, according to Hahn, the Bible was made for liturgical use and liturgical use was the central mark of canonicity for the Scriptures.

Not only are the Scriptures born of and unified by liturgy, but the teachings of Christ himself reinforce the centrality of liturgy. In his exhortation to "do this in remembrance of me," Hahn sees Jesus intentionally referencing the Old Testament liturgical traditions from Jeremiah and Exodus.[78] In fact, it is not just the Scriptures, the so-called Old and New Testaments, that are bound together in a perfect unity, but in fact all of history. "All of salvation history," by which he means to include the whole tradition of the Church throughout the ages, "can be seen as leading to the liturgy, to the sacraments."[79]

Such a unity can be demonstrated by the changelessness of the liturgy throughout the ages, Hahn argues. While there are features that may evolve over the history of the Church, he claims in his book on Revelation, *The Lamb's Supper*, that a testament to the power of the Catholic liturgy is the fact that a first-century Christian could walk into today's Mass or one of us into theirs and immediately recognize that same Christian worship taking place. In fact, by simply replacing the trumpets of the liturgical depiction offered in Revelation with the organs most often found in modern Catholic Masses, we see the contemporary Mass present in the early Church.[80]

The liturgy and the Scriptures naturally direct us toward our last central element of Hahn's theological vision, *conversion*. While recognizing that conversion is not just a matter of the intellect, Hahn places heavy emphasis

---

70. Hahn, *Letter and Spirit*, 37.
71. Hahn, *Letter and Spirit*, 38.
72. Hahn, *Letter and Spirit*, 41.
73. Hahn, *Letter and Spirit*, 42.
74. Hahn, *Letter and Spirit*, 42.
75. Hahn, *Letter and Spirit*, 44.
76. Hahn, *Letter and Spirit*, 45.
77. Hahn, *Letter and Spirit*, 46.
78. Hahn, *Consuming the Word*, 22.
79. Hahn, *Letter and Spirit*, 115.
80. Hahn, *The Lamb's Supper*, 120.

on the discipline of apologetics. His *Reasons to Believe*, for instance, argues for the importance of apologetics, both today and in the whole of the Christian tradition, maintaining that the philosophical defense of the faith to nonbelievers is one the most important tools of evangelization and that it is the obligation of every Christian. In defense of this position, Hahn first references 1 Peter 3:15. As he quotes it, the text reads, "Always be prepared to make a defense to any one who calls you to account for the hope that is in you yet do so with gentleness and reverence." Falling in line with his conviction, discussed above, that the Christian must always "be prepared," Hahn compels his audience to become familiar with arguments for the existence of God as well as the unique truth of the Catholic faith.

Hahn begins his discussion of apologetics, in particular, and conversion, in general, with a brief discussion of Thomas Aquinas's Five Ways. Every Catholic has an obligation, born specifically of 1 Peter 3:15, to be able to offer persuasively cosmological, teleological, and moral arguments for God's existence. "The things we see in the world do not arise suddenly out of nothing," Hahn provides as an example, "[yet], an infinite chain of derivation is unthinkable, absurd."[81] And while he personally does not find it persuasive, he thinks it would also be useful to be familiar with Pascal's Wager.[82] He also offers an overview of aesthetic arguments as well as arguments from the reality of numbers and the laws of logic.[83] In fact, he believes that the laws of logic as well as those of mathematics indicates that the atheist is already affirming the immaterial and, thus, might already be on their way to theism if offered further explanation and argumentation.[84] Hahn ends his discussion regarding God's existence with an argument from miracles and prophecy.

81. Hahn, *Reasons to Believe*, 33.

82. Pascal's Wager is the famous argument attributed to Blaise Pascal (although there is some debate as to whether or not he ever intended it as an argument as such), which states that, in the case in which the evidence for God's existence and nonexistence is perceived as being equal, if a believer is wrong and God does not in fact exist, the price of their misbelief is non-existence. If the nonbeliever is wrong and God actually does exist, the price of their misbelief is the wrath and judgment of God. If the believer is correct and God exists, they gain the eternity of heaven. If the nonbeliever is correct and God does not exist, they simply gain nonexistence. Thus, the only possibility of gain and avoidance of pain is to believe, even if in error.

83. Hahn, *Reasons to Believe*, 23.

84. Hahn, *Reasons to Believe*, 24. "Materialists, objectivists, and empiricists may be well on their way to the kingdom. As we show them the layers of the universe—even in the natural order—we are preparing them to understand the sacramentality of creation." It is of further interest that Hahn uses "materialists, objectivists, and empiricists" in contrast to Christians given that there are Christians who, though qualified in a variety of ways, would also describe themselves with one or all of these designations.

Here again, however, there are aspects of Hahn's discussion that will need to be addressed. First and foremost, there is an interesting exegetical element to Hahn's employment of 1 Peter 3:15. This passage he renders, "Always be prepared to make a defense to any one who calls you to account for the hope that is in you yet do so with gentleness and reverence." That same passage, appearing on the USCCB's copy of the Scriptures, is presented as, "Always be prepared to give an explanation to anyone who asks you for a reason for your hope, but do so with gentleness and reverence."[85] Granted, the fourth version of the New American Bible Revised Edition was published in 2011, yet the rendering of this verse has not changed from the 1986 edition. Given that the NABRE is employed by the USCCB website and the 1986 NAB by the Vatican website, it is important that we ask why Hahn chose the Revised Standard Version when the NAB would be more familiar to his Catholic faithful readership. It is also unclear as to why he provides no reference to this disparity between the translation he chose and the one utilized by the remainder of the Church.

After all, there is a fundamentally different connotation at play here. When we are asked to give an explanation "for the reason for your hope," how many of us respond with the teleological argument for God's existence rather than an account of how Christ and the Church have moved in your life? Further, when Hahn goes on to discuss Aquinas's Five Ways, he leaves out the salient point that Aquinas himself describes the purpose of the Five Ways as a means of strengthening the faith of believers, and not for the purposes of apologetics and evangelization. In fact, Aquinas, in a section of *Rationibus Fidei* entitled "How to argue with nonbelievers," discourages believers from attempting to prove Catholic doctrine to the nonbeliever, as it will be nonsense to those who are without faith and to do so "would belittle the sublimity of the Faith."[86] And while Hahn never mentions Anselm in *Reasons to Believe*, Anselm offers a similar warning in regards to the now famously misnamed ontological "argument."[87]

Hahn also offers Justin Martyr's *Apologies* as evidence that present day Catholics should be engaged in the discipline of apologetics. In *Reasons to Believe*, Hahn employs philosophical and theological argument for the

---

85. 1 Peter 3:15.

86. Aquinas, *Rationibus Fidei*.

87. The *Proslogion*, in which Anselm offers his now famous ontological argument, is titled in English with the hallmark of Anselm's approach, "Faith Seeking Understanding." It is evident from the Introduction to the *Proslogion* that Anselm never intended his discussion to be the sort of discourse that could be employed to convince the nonbeliever. His defining of God as "that being than which no greater can be conceived" was offered as a prayer and not as a kind of apologetics.

purposes of conversion: "We're looking for answers that will satisfy—first ourselves and then others," Hahn writes. "[But if] our defense does not flow from deep preparation, deep Christian formation, it will be unconvincing at best, but merely offensive at worst."[88] When we look at Martyr's *Apologies*, however, we do not see someone who is seeking to win over his interlocutors with proofs of Christianity, but rather someone seeking to correct the record regarding how the Christian community is perceived. Martyr is demanding evidence from the Romans that the Christians are as evil, perverted, and uninformed as they have suggested, otherwise their attacks against Christians must abandoned.[89] What Martyr significantly does not do is endorse anything that looks anything like Hahn's "the best defense is a good offense" approach to apologetics, which he endorses in the introduction to the book.[90] His rendering of 1 Peter 3:15 in support of this apologetical mode, despite the writings of Justin Martyr, the teachings of Thomas Aquinas, or the example of the Church, can only be regarded as in the service of Hahn's overarching project, which, at least in this regard, is at tension with the tradition.

Following the exhortation to become proficient in Christian apologetics, Hahn moves to biblical proofs of the unique truth of the Catholic faith. Here, he provides argument to the effect that evangelical *sola scriptura* is both self-referentially incoherent as well as always contradicted by the actual doctrines and traditions that are celebrated within particular Protestant communions.[91] He also demonstrates the rightness of the Catholic faith from the notion that Paul refers to the Church as one body. In response to the notion that Paul might have simply been speaking figuratively or spiritually, Hahn notes that Paul would surely have chosen something other than "body," perhaps "soul," if he was interested in teaching the Church was metaphorically one body.[92] He provides brief accounts of apostolicity, hagiology, Mariology, and liturgy that all lead to the conclusion that the Catholic Church is the Church Christ began in Peter. Hahn reinforces the importance of apologetics in his discussion of Mary in his, *Hail, Holy Queen*. There he concludes that the author of the Gospel of Matthew was offering a "preemptive apologetic strike," by citing women in Jesus' genealogy. "For surely the

---

88. Hahn, *Reasons to Believe*, 12.

89. Justin Martyr, *First Apology*, 7. "For we have come, not to flatter you by this writing, nor please you by our address, but to beg that you pass judgment [sc. of the Christian's immorality], after an accurate and searching investigation . . . ."

90. Hahn, *Reasons to Believe*, 12.

91. Hahn, *Reasons to Believe*, 69–70.

92. Hahn, *Reasons to Believe*, 79.

evangelist knew," Hahn concludes, "that the claim of Jesus' virginal conception would evoke wry smiles from skeptics."[93]

This emphasis that Hahn places on apologetics provides us with an insight into his understanding of conversion. In his own walk of faith, Hahn was first converted to Christian (though non-Catholic) belief through the work of another apologetics and evangelism ministry, Young Life.[94] Yet, it was alone in his bedroom, poring over the Scriptures, that the young Hahn learned to "[fall] in love with the Word of God."[95] With regard to his conversion to Catholicism, Hahn cites both the hours spent alone filling out notebooks in Marquette's library as well as his time sitting by himself at the back of Mass for the first time.[96] While both conversions take place within the context of education, the first, learning from a couple of Young Life leaders, and the second, during his time in Marquette University's doctoral program, are also deeply personal and individual assents to research he performed himself. While understanding Catholicism as a community of the faithful, Hahn maintains that in the Eucharist one is accepting Christ as their "personal Lord and Savior."[97] A proficiency in apologetics is critical, then, as it is in intellectual assent that the nonbeliever first accepts the truth, in the solitariness of their minds before God.

It was at the age of fifteen, when his classics teacher encouraged his conversion to evangelicalism, that Blessed John Henry Newman made the nominal Anglicanism of his faith his own.[98] According to Newman, his conversion was the recognition that despite his own intellectual acumen, his abilities were insufficient to allow him to live the life of virtue he sought. Newman eventually settled in the more traditional and intellectually interested Anglican communion.[99] It was as an Anglican that Newman became a priest and professor. Unknowingly, he also placed himself in the midst of an intense religious conflict between the stilted religious discourse, practice, and skepticism of the Anglican academic elite and the subjective, anti-intellectual spirituality of Protestant Liberal Evangelicalism.

As a theologian, Newman wrote continuously in defense of three fundamental propositions, the first being that dogma is the foundation of

---

93. Hahn, *Hail, Holy Queen*, 75.
94. Hahn, "The Scott Hahn Conversion Story."
95. Hahn, *Rome Sweet Home*, 5.
96. Hahn, *The Fourth Cup*, 155.
97. Hahn, *Reasons to Believe*, 71.
98. Short, *Newman and His Family*, 33.
99. Bouyer, *Newman*, 27.

Christianity.[100] The thrust of the liberal Protestantism with which Newman saw himself in conflict was a rejection of dogma for the sake of the primacy of subjective religious experience. This particular Protestant ideology sought to hold the personal in higher esteem than the ecclesial, claiming that the Holy Spirit is at work more in the lives of the individual than in the universal Church. His second conviction was that there was such a thing as a visible Church, with sacraments and rites through which we receive grace, and that, "this was the doctrine of Scripture, of the early Church, and of the Anglican Church."[101] And last, he defended the notion that there should be a strict adherence to the Episcopal system as laid out in the Epistles of St. Ignatius and reinforced in the Thirty-Nine Articles, the defining tenets of the Episcopal communion.[102]

It was in regard to these Thirty-Nine Articles, however, that Newman first found himself at odds with the Anglican hierarchy. In his Tract 90, Newman forcefully laid out his thesis that the Thirty-Nine Articles can and ought to be read in the most Catholic sense possible. Newman began his tract with the bold claim, "It is a duty which we owe both to the Catholic Church, and to our own, to take our reformed confession in the most Catholic sense they will admit: we have no duties towards their framers."[103] Yet, the reception of his tract by both the Anglican religious hierarchy and the Oxford intellectuals was intensely critical. In fact, the critiques against the tract as well as against Newman himself were so brutal that in the aftermath of its publication he despaired that he had lost everything.

Nevertheless, Newman became increasingly convinced that his interpretation of Anglicanism was accurate. What he described as the *via media*, or middle way, contained all of the richness of the Roman Catholic tradition, without the ills of "Romish" superstition and idolatry that plagued the Catholic communion. His readers, however, saw in his writings a defense of Roman Catholicism and an attempt to undermine Anglicanism. Newman never actually intended such a thing but had inadvertently painted himself into a corner in his critique of contemporary Anglicanism.[104]

His sympathy for the Roman tradition, however, had finally firmly ensnared him, even if his reason was still desperately clinging to some form

---

100. Newman, *Apologia Pro Vita Sua*, 61.
101. Newman, *Apologia Pro Vita Sua*, 62.
102. Newman, *Apologia Pro Vita Sua*, 62.
103. Newman, *Apologia Pro Vita Sua*, 127.
104. Turner, *John Henry Newman*, 198. Turner carries this idea further to claim that Newman was forced into his conversion to Catholicism by the response to his Tractarian writings as well as certain relationships that had become strained and bombastic by the 1840s. For a critique of this position, see also Cunningham, "John Henry Newman."

of Anglo-Catholicism, and his audience made it clear that even this weaker Romanism had no place among Anglican intellectuals. In this singular event, Newman saw his life work as well as his identity as a faithful Anglican taken from him. He wrote his bishop in Oxford, under heavy pressure by the Oxford clergy and intellectuals to either recant or leave, and resigned.

Even in the chaos of his world falling apart, Newman remained committed to discovering the true Church founded by Jesus Christ in his world:

> The one question was, what was I to do? I had to make up my mind for myself, and others could not help me. I determined to be guided, not by my imagination, but by my reason. And this I said over and over again in the years which followed, both in conversation and in private letters. . . . Moreover, I felt on consideration a positive doubt, on the other hand, whether the suggestion did not come from below. Then I said to myself, Time alone can solve that question.[105]

The ellipses in the quote above, however, passed over something incredibly important. In the midst of recounting his search for truth, Newman confessed, "Had it not been for this severe resolve, I should have been a Catholic sooner than I was."[106]

Newman would go on to become one of the great theological voices of Catholic history. His genius forever changed the Catholic Church. By his own account, however, if it were not for his own pride, his reliance on his own genius, his commitment to "make up my mind for myself," he would have found his way to the Church earlier. In the end, he left a book unfinished, gave over his prideful belief in his absolute self-sufficiency, and turned to "a simple holy man," a local priest, "and [asked] of him admission into the One Fold of Christ."[107]

Had it not been for Bl. Newman's and St. Augustine's self-confessed severe resolve to find the truth for themselves, if they had turned earlier to the simple, quiet wisdom of a local parish priest or the compassionate strength of friends, they both would have found their way to the truth more quickly. Where then, in the story of his own journey of faith, does Hahn, like Saint Augustine and Blessed John Henry Newman, turn away from confidence in his own abilities to fall upon the wisdom and strength of others?

---

105. Newman, *Apologia Pro Vita Sua*, 118.
106. Newman, *Apologia Pro Vita Sua*, 118.
107. Newman, *Apologia Pro Vita Sua*, 211.

2

Revelation's Gift of the Mass

In 1974, Jacques Derrida published his now famous *Of Grammatology*. Here, Derrida noted that the simple actions of reading and writing are significantly more complex than we had been led to believe. In writing, we seem to assume a one-to-one correspondence between the ideas that we are seeking to convey and the words that we put on the page. We believe that through writing we simply and perfectly connect the ideas of our minds, the words we write on a page, and the aspects of the external world that we are seeking to address. Derrida reminds us, however, that there is more to writing that we commonly allow. "[The] writer," he offers, "writes *in* a language and *in* a logic whose proper system, laws, and life his discourse by definition cannot dominate absolutely."[1] This process of transferring thoughts to page would be simple, that is, but for the fact that we employ a language that we are born into. The vocabulary, grammar, idioms, and oddities of the English language were bestowed upon us (imperfectly) by a history, culture, and society that we can never fully understand. An author only uses these tools properly when they allow themselves to be "used by the system."[2] Moreover, writing is performed at specific places and particular times.

The difficulties double when one moves from writing to reading. In the case of reading, the words that made it onto the page were the complex result of an author's intention and their particular mastery of the language, their place within society, and their appropriation of culture. Moreover, this

---

1. Derrida, *Of Grammatology*, 158.
2. Derrida, *Of Grammatology*, 158.

complex of environmental, linguistic, social, and cultural embeddedness carries us into particular channels of expression in ways that are often completely invisible to us. That is, while our experience is one of writing in a language, it is more accurate to describe this process as language writing us. Those same aspects are present in the case of the reader, yet the reader is in even less of a position to fully master the text given that the distance between themselves and the text that they are reading is mirrored in the distance between the text and the author. Despite our assumptions to the contrary, in reading the reader is necessarily unable to reproduce "[the] conscious, voluntary, intentional relationship that the writer institutes in his exchanges with the history to which he belongs thanks to the element of language." Reading, for Derrida, then, is always more akin to commentary than reproduction, and it is this that makes reading, as he describes it, a task. Further, it is a task that we all too often oversimplify to our detriment. "To recognize and respect all the classical exigencies is not easy," Derrida cautions, "and requires all the instruments of traditional criticism."[3] So while Derrida's exegetical strategy could hardly be described as itself neither "classical" nor "traditional," he does recognize the role that traditional criticism has played. The mistakes of traditional modes of reading do not lie so much in their construction but in their application. The "indispensable guardrail" of literary criticism that has acted to protect text from losing all sense of meaning has, according to Derrida, "only *protected*, never *opened*, a reading."[4]

At the risk of appearing to have *opened* Derrida's text, Derrida is in short asking us, in the face of the deep history of both ourselves and the text, to try to be self-reflective about the fact that we cannot possibly remember or even recognize all that we bring with us to a text or all that a text carries with it. Despite our common assumption that our beliefs are formed in some sort of abstraction and properly map on to a static and uninterpreted external world, we view the world, texts, and even traditions through the lens of ourselves and our historical-cultural embeddedness. Every confession of belief, summary of another's intellectual contributions, and act of writing is itself a revelation into the assumptions, prejudices, and biases of the individual. Accessing an author's intention, human or divine, is something that we can only ever gesture towards, and the more we attempt to disregard the complex task of critical reading the less likely we are to arrive at anything approximating it. The reading of any text, including the Holy Scriptures, then, is an act of faith and an exercise in patience and humility.

3. Derrida, *Of Grammatology*, 158.
4. Derrida, *Of Grammatology*, 158.

Scott Hahn's *The Lamb's Supper* is not straightforwardly a book on Scripture as much as it is a thesis concerning the connection between the Mass and the New Testament book of Revelation. It is, however, an excellent resource for examining his use of Scripture. The work rests upon the "outlandish" notion that while Revelation is notoriously difficult to interpret, the "key to understanding the Mass is the biblical Book of Revelation—and, further, that the Mass is the only way a Christian can truly makes sense of the Book of Revelation."[5]

Before proceeding, it is important to unpack this initial claim. First and foremost, Hahn recognizes the seemingly unorthodox approach (he will go on to argue that his take is in fact that of the tradition) of linking together the book of Revelation and the Mass. In this opening statement, Hahn recognizes that he is offering something new in this exegetical (and liturgical) approach. Second, Hahn suggests an exegetical approach of viewing portions of Scripture through the lens of Christian practice. What needs to be investigated further is whether Hahn is claiming that this was the intention of the author in writing Revelation, or some underlying aim in the inspiration by the Holy Spirit, or something else entirely. Third, it is important to note that Hahn sees that the Scriptures in general can, to some degree, be seen as the "key" to unlocking the meaning and purposes of the Mass and, conversely, that the Scriptures, in part, can be unlocked by viewing it through the lens of Christian practice.

What guides Hahn in all of this is the centrality of tradition in the Catholic faith. As will become clear as we proceed, Hahn places a massive emphasis on tradition; he does not just allow it to inform his work but sees himself as simply repeating tradition. Hahn never makes explicit exactly how he understands tradition here, but in his *The First Society*, he offers:

> [The Church] exists in the here and now, but also reaches backward and forward in a *unity through time* that is unique among human institutions. In so doing, she provides a more solid foundation for social order than any other organization or ideology every could.[6]

Tradition for Hahn, then, is that unity through time that maintains the unchanging faith that has remained undivided and unchanged from its inception.[7] Thus, a tension that Hahn must resolve by the conclusion of his discussion is the apparent "outlandishness" of his original thesis in light

---

5. Hahn, *The Lamb's Supper*, 4.
6. Hahn, *The First Society*, 77, emphasis added.
7. Hahn, *Reasons to Believe*, 79.

of the unchanging nature of the faith. That is, Hahn, according to his own understanding of the nature of the Church and Church teaching, cannot be offering anything new to the timeless tradition of the Catholic faith.

Hahn continues with the caveat that his book on Revelation and the Mass "is not a 'Bible study.'"[8] He describes his effort as a practical application of a single aspect of Revelation, and by no means an exhaustive exegesis. In so doing, Hahn claims to be leaving aside the academic questions of authorship or time period; as he understands Revelation as a mystical book, such questions should not be seen as primary. To this end, Hahn distances himself from his former approach as an evangelical interpreter of Scripture, whom he describes as looking for encoded messages about the end times or what worship might look like in heaven in the hereafter. In understanding Revelation as a mystical text, a concept that will need to be unpacked at some point, Hahn understands himself as deviating from the Calvinist, evangelical exegetical approach of his pre-Catholic life of faith. Yet, the characteristics of his current approach here are a little more difficult to determine.

While Hahn speaks much more definitively concerning that which his methodology is not, there are a few places where he provides clues to how he understands his approach. Quoting Joseph Ratzinger, before he became Pope Benedict XVI, Hahn formally connects the interpretation of the Scriptures with the development of Catholic doctrine: "Dogma is by definition nothing other than an interpretation of Scripture . . . which has sprung from the faith over the centuries."[9] As he makes evident throughout his work in a variety of different contexts, Hahn understands himself to be merely describing the testimony of the tradition rather than providing any particularly new insight himself. And while the variety of exegetical approaches throughout the history of the Church makes such a claim difficult to substantiate, his statement here at the very least begins to indicate the importance of Ratzinger's approach to Scripture on Hahn's interpretive vision.

While he makes clear the heavy emphasis he places upon Ratzinger's scriptural exegesis, an exegetical approach that Ratzinger has written about a great length, Hahn rarely makes such reliance explicit in his discussion of Scripture passages themselves. During a discussion of the "Do this in remembrance of Me"[10] from the Eucharistic prayer, Hahn offers the following regarding the importance of God "remembering His covenant":

---

8. Hahn, *The Lamb's Supper*, 5.

9. Hahn, *The Lamb's Supper*, 50. Originally found in Joseph Ratzinger, "Crisis in Catechesis," 8.

10. I Corinthians 11:25

In the Old Testament, for example, we often read that God "remembered His covenant." Well, it's not as if He could ever forget His covenant; but at certain times, for the benefit of His people, He reenacted it. That's what He does, through His priest, in the remembrance of the Mass. He makes His covenant new once again.[11]

God's covenant with God's people is, of course, given a central place in the Old Testament story, yet what is of interest for the current discussion is Hahn's alluding to Old Testament stories that notably play a complicated and important role in Catholic theology without him feeling the need to explain or even provide the actual references for the stories in the Scriptures for his readers. Such a decision might give rise to the idea among his readers that Hahn perceives the scriptural account as largely straightforward, accessible, and simple. An exegetical position that would be in tension with the scriptural assumptions present in Ratzinger's work.

Turning to his examination of Revelation itself, we find Hahn's earlier disinterest in questions of dating and authorship has changed.[12] Hahn briefly takes up the question of the date of Revelation's writing. "Almost all agree," he writes, "that John's measurement of the Temple (Rev. 11:1) points to a pre-70 date, since after 70 there would have been no Temple to measure."[13] It is, first, important to note that there is nothing approaching any kind of a consensus on this dating of the book of Revelation among either ecclesial or scholarly discussion. Further, it is very difficult indeed to find any interpreter of Revelation at all who holds to a pre-70 AD date who does so for the reason Hahn offers. More often than not, claims of consensus among scholars offered in lieu of sufficient argumentation simply reveals a scholar's preferred sources rather than a depiction of any kind of scholarly reality.

Hahn also then takes up the question of Revelation's author. Hahn confesses that there has been and continues to be significant disagreement concerning the authorship of Revelation. Despite claiming that such a debate is "incidental" to his discussion, however, Hahn goes on to offer argument as to not only why the apostle John is the author, but, moreover, why such a distinction matters. Hahn, rightly, first establishes that there is a clear textual association with John and the author of the Apocalypse in, for instance, Revelation 1:4, 9, and 22:8. Here again, however, his argument includes a somewhat unconventional element. In seeking to align the author of Revelation with that of John's Gospel, incidentally another book

11. Hahn, *The Lamb's Supper*, 54.
12. Hahn, *The Lamb's Supper*, 5.
13. Hahn, *The Lamb's Supper*, 70.

whose author is in question, he points to the John of Revelation's familiarity with the specifics of the Temple and Jerusalem. Given the Gospel of John's employment of the title, "Lamb of God," linking these two books together under the authorship of the Beloved Disciple, John, furthers Hahn's contention that the phrase "Lamb of God" stands as the core of understanding the book of Revelation as well as the Mass. As Hahn relies upon this aspect of Revelation as evidence that the book should be viewed through the lens of the Mass (and vice versa), what Hahn first describes as "incidental" by the end of his brief discussion becomes the cornerstone of his central argument.

More critical for our purposes, however, is Hahn's presentation of the available exegetical approaches for Revelation. Historically, there have been no end of interpreters who have tried to make sense of Revelation's depiction of the Temple and the host of characters involved in the scene. Hahn, here, focuses on four that he regards as somewhat exhausting the exegetical space: futurists, preterists, idealists, and historicists. What he names the "futurists" are those approaches that claim to have found Napoleon, Bismarck, Hitler, and Stalin as well as God's plan for the ultimate end of the world in Revelation's pages. The "preterists" read the apocalypse as a warning against first-century Roman emperors. "Idealists" read Revelation as an allegory for the spiritual battle every believer must fight in their life of faith. And the "historicist" sees in Revelation's complicated pages a symbolic depiction of the entirety of human history.[14] Which, then, does Hahn endorse? The interesting answer Hahn provides is, "Well, all of them. There's no reason they can't all be simultaneously true."[15]

Here then, we find that Hahn is willing to accept, at least partially, what is more often a fundamentalist interpretation of Revelation that identifies end-times antichrists, spiritual battles, and prophecies. While he does confess a preference for the preterist approach, Hahn expresses concern with discounting the others. "What binds them all together," Hahn writes, "is what binds us all to Christ: the New Covenant, sealed and renewed by the Eucharistic liturgy."[16] After all, he contends, while the preterist holds that the Apocalypse describes a very specific period of history, the Scriptures as a whole must always also apply to the entirety of history; that is, to that most mysterious last period of history, also.

What unites these different interpretations of Revelation together in a Catholic context, if Hahn is correct, is the Eucharistic liturgy, which entails

14. Hahn is not alone in his depiction of these four interpretive approaches. The designations of futurists, preterists, idealists, and historicists are somewhat common among evangelical discussions of Revelation, but not overly common elsewhere.

15. Hahn, *The Lamb's Supper*, 73.

16. Hahn, *The Lamb's Supper*, 73.

that for any interpretation there must be some degree of participation in the tradition. Otherwise, any approach that any Christian took concerning Revelation at any time would have just as much legitimacy as the four presented above. What remains to be demonstrated, however, is that each of these four are strongly visible in the tradition. Yet, the futurist perspective is one that has been most often discussed among those Evangelicals who believe that we are today living in the end times. An examination of Catholic encyclical tradition, for instance, demonstrates that while the many different approaches to Revelation are discussed, the futurist interpretation of the Apocalypse of John is quite simply not offered as a defensible interpretation.[17]

What is more interesting, however, is that Hahn offers the following from Joseph Ratzinger, his most important influence, in the notes for this section of the book:

> On this basis, we can offer a faithful evaluation of the language of cosmic symbolism in the New Testament. This language is liturgical.... [This] analysis allows us to draw two conclusions. The cosmic imagery of the New Testament cannot be used as a source for the description of a future chain of cosmic events. *All attempts of this kind are misplaced.*[18]

Given this claim, it is hard to imagine that Ratzinger would accept the possibility of a futurist approach that Hahn here defends. This is a serious challenge to the notion that Hahn does nothing more in his works than repeat accepted Catholic tradition.

Moving on to Hahn's actual exegetical journey through the Apocalypse, keeping in mind his willingness to countenance a futurist interpretation, we now must examine the different figures and themes Hahn identifies. The first figure at whom we take a closer look is "the woman clothed with the sun." Here, his argument is much more straightforwardly traditionally Catholic in that he identifies this woman as Mary, which in turn places Mary as of crucial importance to the apocalyptic and soteriological connotations of Revelation. Recorded in Revelation 11:19,[19] John's vision includes

---

17. Pius XII's *Summi Pontificatus* (1939) employs Revelation to demonstrate the disparity between technological and social progress in the face of communal and spiritual stagnation. John Paul II's *Redemptoris Mater* (1987) discusses the Apocalypse in order to demonstrate Mary's centrality in God's work of salvation. But in neither of these letters, nor any other that I could find, is the Apocalypse presented in a manner commensurate with the futurist's mode of employing Revelation to unlock the specific details of the end of the world.

18. Hahn, *The Lamb's Supper*, 168, emphasis added.

19. Revelation 11:19, "Then God's temple in heaven was opened, and the ark of his covenant could be seen in the temple. There were flashes of lightnings, rumblings, and peals of thunder, an earthquake, and a violent hailstorm."

the opening of God's Temple in heaven and the ark of the covenant lying within. As the discussion of the "woman clothed with the sun" follows this image in chapter 12, Hahn argues for the identification of the ark of the covenant with the woman, who is Mary. In itself, this is not necessarily an overly controversial identification, but Hahn phrases it thus: "I believe (with the Fathers of the Church) that when John describes the woman, he is describing the ark—of the New Covenant."[20] Yet, frustratingly, Hahn provides nothing with which to identify the Church Fathers to whom he is referring.

Such an omission is particularly troubling here as it seems that the present discussion stands at the core of Hahn's argument. By identifying Mary with the ark of the covenant, Hahn seeks to cast the Old Testament description of the ark as an indication of how we should view Mary in Revelation. Hahn reminds us that the ark of the covenant was said to contain the stone tablets give to Moses on which God carved the Law, manna, and Aaron's rod. Mary as the new ark contained within her the Word of God, the Bread of Life, and the eternal high priest, all in the person of Jesus Christ. While such a connection between Mary and the covenant is certainly convenient for the purposes of Hahn's argument, given the gravity of such an identification and the role it plays in his argument, not providing the specific Fathers who make such an identification prevents us from examining if they took the analogy as straightforwardly descriptive as Hahn does here.[21]

He moves from his discussion of Revelation's depiction of Mary to an investigation of the infamous beasts of John's vision. Hahn begins by confessing an "urgency" to impress upon us that the beasts summoned by the great dragon of Revelation are more than simply symbols. "They are real spiritual beings," Hahn writes, "members of the satanic 'lowerarchy,' demonic persons who have controlled and corrupted the political destiny of nations."[22] It is, of course, a rather innocuous Catholic claim to argue for the reality of Satan and his minions. The Catechism of the Catholic Church, for instance, describes the fall of Satan and his angels in very historical terms and makes it very evident that the Church holds these beings to still be at work in the world, promoting evil and sowing strife and discord.[23] This is not to say, however, that the monsters of John's vision all correlate to specific demonic persons. It is an even greater claim to suggest that these demonic realities have "controlled and corrupted" the political destiny of nations.

---

20. Hahn, *The Lamb's Supper*, 77.

21. Hahn does offer notes at the end of the book regarding this discussion, yet there are no citations to specific Church Fathers here either.

22. Hahn, *The Lamb's Supper.*, 80.

23. "The Fall of the Angels" in *The Catechism of the Catholic Church*, §391.

In support of his claims here, Hahn makes reference[24] to the Sacred Congregation for the Doctrine of the Faith's "Christian Faith and Demonology." While the document does contain the notion that "by revealing the enigma of the different names and symbols of Satan in Scripture definitively unmasks his identity," it in no way indicates that the reader is to assume that each of the beasts here mentioned should be understood as identifying specific members of the demonic court.[25] Such an issue is important here because Hahn employs it to fit the continued narrative of Revelation and the Mass. For Revelation to be what he is suggesting it is, then every part of the book needs to have some correlation to either the Mass or those who are coming to the Mass. If our actions in the Mass are united with, as Hahn puts it, "unseen heavenly things," then our sinful actions are connected to the efforts of Satan and his demons.[26] Revelation, just as it gifts us with a cosmic reality to the activities of the Mass, demonstrates the reality behind the state of sin in the world. The first beast, which has seven heads and ten horns, Hahn, noting the fact that it wears a crown on every horn, identifies as representing "all corrupted political authority" as well as the "corrupting spiritual force" behind any corrupt government.[27]

It is important to pause here and make note of precisely the claims being made in this brief analysis. First, Hahn makes it clear that, at the very least, for every beast or monster mentioned in Revelation, there is a specific demonic reality residing behind it. What is not clear is how exactly Hahn claims that we know such a thing. As has been discussed previously, it is evident that both the Scriptures and the tradition of the Church attest to the reality of both angels and demons. That being said, there is very little offered to the Church in aid of identifying specific supernatural entities. Second, in identifying the first beast as "corrupted political authority" and then suggesting that it represents the "corrupting spiritual force" that lies behind any corrupt government, Hahn appears to be suggesting that every corrupt government is so because it is in the grip of the demonic. It is incredibly problematic, however, to suggest that any government that is not acting according to the edicts of God, or more importantly, any government that *I deem* to not be acting according to the edicts of God, is being controlled by the literal minions of evil.

This position is troubling, however, for another important reason. Throughout *The Lamb's Supper*, Hahn argues not only that his approach is

---

24. This reference is found only in the "Notes" section at the end of his book.
25. Sacred Congregation for the Doctrine of the Faith, "Christian Faith and Demonology," (1975).
26. Hahn, *The Lamb's Supper*, 80.
27. Hahn, *The Lamb's Supper*, 81–82.

the one that is proper, but also that it is the approach found in the tradition. As discussed previously, it is not clear that Hahn is as successful in this as he might think with his references to "the Fathers," etc. This critique notwithstanding, he does make it evident that he recognizes the importance of providing evidence for the claims that one makes. In this final assertion, that any government deemed to not be acting in accordance with the edicts of God is being controlled by the demonic, it is not at all clear what kind of evidence could be provided to justify such a massive and horrific claim. While Christianity in general, and Catholicism more specifically, rejects the epistemological demands of logical positivism,[28] the tradition has maintained the importance of some kind of religious epistemological satisfaction. That is, it matters that we do not make pronouncements without also providing the appropriate evidence for their truth. The claim that literal demonic persons are controlling specific corrupt governments sets a precedent for declaring beliefs without any degree of epistemological satisfaction.

Returning to the text, Hahn continues his discussion by attempting to identify another beast mentioned in Revelation. This beast is described as coming out of the earth and having horns like a lamb. Here, Hahn recognizes in the description of the beast the "corrupted priesthood in first-century Jerusalem."[29] This corrupted priesthood, in handing over Christ to the Roman authorities, certainly does seem to have been acting like a beast in a lamb's clothing, to borrow Hahn's language, yet the following claim stretches the metaphor further than we should be comfortable:

> So they rejected Christ and elevated Caesar. They rejected the Lamb and worshipped the beast. Certainly Caesar was the government's ruler and as such deserved respect. . . . *But Caesar wanted more than respect. He demanded sacrificial worship, which the chief priests gave him when they handed over the Lamb of God.*[30]

As far as we can tell, Caesar was entirely absent from the events surrounding Jesus' death; while it is rhetorically pleasing to depict these corrupt

---

28. Logical positivism, a philosophical position made popular in the early twentieth century by analytic philosophers, is the position that the only statements that have meaning are those that are either empirically verifiable or analytic. The existence of God, for instance, famously does not fall into either category. The belief then was that the statement "God exists," was not actually false, but rather entirely devoid of any meaning altogether. While it is important that we reject the notion that claims concerning the demonic residing behind corrupt institutions are literal nonsense, it is crucial that we appreciate the weight of epistemological evidence required for such a claim.

29. Hahn, *The Lamb's Supper*, 82.

30. Hahn, *The Lamb's Supper*, 83, emphasis added.

priests as sacrificing the very God they were supposed to be serving to the pinnacle of worldly authority, it is not at all clear how such a move makes any degree of exegetical sense.

Hahn's discussion of the beasts of Revelation comes to a conclusion with that most infamous part of revelations imagery, the number of the beast. Taking a stab at identifying the meaning of the beast's followers receiving the mark on their foreheads, Hahn walks through the now commonplace attempts to connect the number '666' with Nero, the wisdom of Solomon, and the degradation of the number for perfection and the Old Testament covenant, which is seven.[31] He finishes his discussion with an assertion with which all interpreters of Revelation should be in agreement. No matter the approach one takes with the mark of the beast, any interpretation that includes even the smallest degree of anti-Semitism must be rejected.

Having finished with his unpacking of the beasts of the Apocalypse, Hahn turns next to Revelation's angels. Just as with the demonic, Hahn is here ready to take Revelation at its face. The depiction of these mysterious denizens of heaven is rather alarming. Hahn takes the imagery employed and reads it metaphorically. The many eyes of the angels indicate their knowledge and watchfulness while their six wings demonstrate their swiftness and vigilance. Hahn continues, however, by claiming that, in fact, "Though heaven's angels present themselves to human eyes in physical form, angels do not actually have bodies."[32] While the mystery of the angelic has long been of interest for Christians, the level of insight that Hahn claims into their secrets here should strike us as troubling. There are, of course, many places throughout the history of Church where the topic of the angels has been taken up. Thomas Aquinas, in his *Summa Theologiae*, provides a very similar account. In Question 50 of the *Prima Pars*, he takes

---

31. In the "Notes" section at the conclusion of the book, Hahn offers a reference to Austin Farrer's *A Rebirth in Images*. Looking at the pages cited in Farrer, the author does some incredibly sophisticated mathematics, particularly involving triangles, with the number 666 that he offers as a possibility for John's employment of it in the Apocalypse. Farrer concludes this section with the following claim: "The coincidence between this reckoning and the factors of the 666 triangle is no mere accident. St. John's reckoning of the period of the reign is artificial, devised for the sake of conformity with the factors of the 666 triangle.... The purpose of the artificial reckoning is to exhibit the Beast's fatally limited reign as a function of his number." Here then, Farrer makes the claim that John seems to be doing precisely the opposite of what Hahn describes him as doing. Namely, Hahn has been portraying the vision of Revelation as entirely received by John and to be interpreted as such. Yet, Farrer's willingness to talk about the mark of the beast as "artificial" and "devised" appears to render Revelation more in terms of a hermeneutical device employed to perform a Christian message.

32. Hahn, *The Lamb's Supper*, 86.

up questions of the angels' incorporeality, incorruptibility, and number.[33] Yet, there is an important difference between what Aquinas discusses in the *Summa* as compared to what Hahn is offering here.

First, Aquinas recognizes that there are disagreements concerning the details of the angelic from both within and outside of the tradition. He then goes on to provide some argumentation as to why he believes that he is correct. That is, Aquinas presents his discussions of these messengers of God within the context of theological discourse, within which there could be a multitude of views and disagreement even while maintaining that there is a truth of the matter. Hahn's discussion here is presented with a high degree of certainty regarding the angelic. Moreover, Hahn takes the angels as they are specifically mentioned in Revelation and provides a straightforward account of what they mean. Further, he tracks the angelic denizens of Revelation's vision back into those divine visitors of the Old Testament. All this he does without even the hint of a recognition that there is an array of diverse views within the tradition for which even Aquinas's provides in his constant refrain from the *Summa*, "I answer that . . ."

Second, throughout the entirety of the *Summa*, Aquinas never makes any claim regarding the presence of a supernatural being acting in the world with anything approaching the specificity Hahn offers. In Question 108, Article Five of that same part, Aquinas takes up the question of whether angels have named orders, e.g., cherubim, seraphim, etc. Neither Thomas's section on the angels, Questions 50 through 64, nor here in 108, does Thomas attempt to provide the identity of any particular angel not directly named in the Scriptures nor assign to any specific angel a particular order or categorization not given in the Bible. Even the great doctor of the Church, Thomas Aquinas, does not do then what Hahn is attempting here.

Hahn next turns his attention to the "great city" of Revelation that seems to be the aim of Revelation's rebuke. Chapter 11 describes the city as having "the symbolic names "Sodom" and "Egypt," where indeed their Lord was crucified."[34] He claims that this "clearly indicates" that the city of Revelation is Jerusalem. This he then ties to Revelation's later depiction of Babylon in chapters 17–19, presenting the Apocalypse as univocally attacking Jerusalem. Such a conclusion would be reasonable for the casual

---

33. Aquinas, *Summa Theologiae, prima pars*, q. 50, art. 1: "I answer that, there must be some incorporeal creatures. For what is principally intended by God in creatures is good, and this consists in assimilation to God Himself. . . . Now God produces the creature by his intellect. Hence the perfection of the universe requires that there should be intellectual creatures, . . . the perfection of the universe requires the existence of an incorporeal creature."

34. Revelation 11:8.

interpreter of the Bible, yet a cursory investigation of the tradition's examination of the "great city" shows a rather different consensus.

In a paper read to the Society of Biblical Literature at the Pontifical Gregorian University in 2001, Giancarlo Biguzzi took up the question of the identity of this city. Rather than challenging a prevailing notion that this city should be read as Jerusalem, Biguzzi describes the view, held "since antiquity," that the city ought to be recognized as Rome as the "traditional interpretation."[35] Biguzzi goes on to defend this traditional reading and explains in a note that despite being challenged by "some twenty interpreters . . . in recent centuries," it is the appropriate interpretation.[36] Supporting Biguzzi's depiction of Rome as the traditional understanding is the explanation given in both the USCCB's and the Vatican's online presentation of Revelation. According to an explanatory note from the Vatican's online English edition of Revelation, the expression "great city" is "used constantly for in Rev[elation] for Babylon, i.e., Rome . . ." and the phrase "where indeed the Lord was crucified" does not refer to the geographical Jerusalem but the "symbolic Jerusalem that rejects God and his witness, i.e., Rome, called Babylon in Rev[elation] 16–18."[37] Moreover, such a disagreement is not merely some scholarly exegetical squabble, according to Biguzzi, given that allowing Jerusalem to be the city identified would render Revelation "all of a sudden an anti-Jewish libel." Thus, despite being "clear" to Hahn that the city of Revelation 11 and 17–19 is Jerusalem, the Church has traditionally not read it that way and now recognizes that deviating from the tradition in this regard could have damning anti-Semitic implications.

Recognizing this potential difficulty, Hahn soon takes up the question of Revelation as anti-Semitic. To this troubling question, he quickly responds with a "firm no," given that "John's vision makes no sense unless Israel is the firstborn of all nations."[38] We need to be cautious here, however, because despite Hahn's claim, the explanation he provides is, at least, compatible with supersessionism. This is the troubling belief that has haunted Christianity's past, which claims that while the Jews were the firstborn of God, their rejection of Christ has revoked their status as the chosen people of God and rendered their history after the fall of Jerusalem in AD 70 fundamentally unimportant. Hahn's language here, while certainly not intending to encourage any supersessionist exegesis, is insufficient for combating it:

35. Biguzzi, "Is the Babylon of Revelation Rome or Jerusalem?" 386.

36. Biguzzi, "Is the Babylon of Revelation Rome or Jerusalem?" 386.

37. http://www.vatican.va/archive/ENG0839/__P12U.HTM#$54K. The USCCB's online Bible shares similar sentiments regarding the identification of the "great city" and Babylon as Rome.

38. Hahn, *The Lamb's Supper*, 99.

> No, Israel's *defeat* is no cause for celebration. It should cause us to tremble–*because not only can it happen to Christians but it has, repeatedly, and it will likely happen again*. If Israel the firstborn *failed*, so will we, younger siblings, whenever we grow proud and self-reliant.
>
> Thus, I repeat, anti-Semitism and anti-Judaism are spiritually destructive and stupid. In the words of Pope Pius XI: "Spiritually, we are Semites." You cannot be a good Catholic until you've fallen in love with the religion and people of Israel.[39]

While we must agree that a good Catholic must have a love for the religion and people of Israel, talk of Israel's failure and defeat in terms of a warning that we do not want the same to continue to happen to Christians is hardly an explication of that sentiment.

Hahn continues his walk through John's vision by addressing one of the most troubling aspects of Revelation, the wrath of God on the day of Judgment. Here Hahn holds the rather standard position maintaining that the wrath of God is every bit as present in the Scriptures as the love of God and that both are essential to our theological understanding. While admitting that such a theology can at times be emotionally difficult, Hahn offers the notion that we should see the loving hand of God as present even in times of punishment:

> Once we have embraced sin in this way and rejected our covenant with God, only a calamity can save us. Sometimes, the most merciful thing that God can do to a drunk, for example, may be to allow him to wreck his car or be abandoned by his wife— whatever will force him to accept responsibility for his actions. . . .When people read the Apocalypse, they get frightened by the earthquakes and locusts and famines and scorpions. But the only reason that God would all these things is because He loves us.[40]

It must be granted that Hahn is dealing with a very difficult subject matter. The question of God's perfect justice in light of God's omnibenevolence has plagued Christianity since its beginning and so we should not criticize Hahn here for failing to deliver in a handful of paragraphs what the Church is continuing to work out over centuries of thought and prayer. Yet, there is something troubling about the manner by which he connects God's agency with both personal and natural disasters. While there may be a certain logic to the notion that God, as our divine parent, uses the results of our sin to teach and correct, claiming that God allows a "drunk,

39. Hahn, *The Lamb's Supper*, 100, emphasis added.
40. Hahn, *The Lamb's Supper*, 110–11.

for example, to wreck his car or be abandoned by his wife" for the purposes of correcting sinful behavior does little to account for the potential loved one whose life was lost by unfortunately being on the receiving end of a drunk driving accident, nor the grieving wife looking to pick up the pieces of a broken marriage and years of abuse and neglect. Even more troubling is the notion that the Church should turn to the victims of Katrina who ask, "Why God?" and offer, "[The] only reason God would allow these things is because he loves us."[41] The promise of a better world to come should not eclipse the very real suffering endured today.

As closely as Hahn attempts to read these passages concerning beasts and angels, he quickly moves on to the portrayal of humanity present in Revelation. He first notes the importance of the Apocalypse's depiction of "a great multitude" from every nation worshiping God together before the throne of God. It is important that we suspend our modern ecumenically minded religious inclusivism, Hahn exhorts, so that we remember that such an image would have struck the early-Christian reader as scandalous.[42] It seems that here again, however, Hahn is overly quick in his examination. The notion that the Scriptures have been opened to the gentiles has been clear since Matthew's, "Go, therefore, and make disciples of all nations . . . ."[43] The Council of Jerusalem, which scholars date at roughly AD 48, determined that the good news of Christ's salvific work was for all the world and not just the Jews and those converts to Judaism.[44] Even if Hahn's pre-70 dating of Revelation is accurate, this would give the church somewhere in the realm of twenty years to get used to this new understanding of the gentiles. If the date is closer to that provided by the US College of Catholic Bishops' introduction to Revelation,[45] which is 81–96 AD, the fledgling Christian community would have had the better part of fifty years to not just get used to this new idea, but to experience the growing Church as one more globally represented in its membership.

The same is true of Hahn's claim that the reader would have been surprised by these multitudes worshiping before the throne, which Hahn reads as the Holy of Holies. After all, the Synoptic Gospels all include the account of the "veil of the sanctuary," which had separated the Holy of Holies from the rest of the Temple, tearing completely in half. And while the dating of

---

41. Hahn, *The Lamb's Supper*, 111.

42. Hahn, *The Lamb's Supper*, 87.

43. Matthew 28:19—"Go, therefore, and make disciples of all nations, baptizing them in the name of the Father, and of the Son, and of the Holy Spirit."

44. Acts 15:1–29.

45. http://www.usccb.org/bible/revelation/0

the Gospels is also still in some question, they indicate that the story had to have been part of the early-Church consciousness for quite some time. This demonstrates that Revelation's depiction of this liturgical event was meant to reinforce, rather than introduce, a theological commitment.

Finally, Hahn takes up the conclusion to Revelation. The Lamb of God returns in the face of war, famine, death, and destruction to avenge his servants. A figure named "Faithful and True" fights against the powers of darkness with a sword in its mouth, an obvious metaphor for the Scriptures. Hahn relies upon this bizarre depiction to call into question some of the recent portrayals of Christ's second coming. He suggests that instead of a vengeful God returning power to annihilate his enemies, that we should look for the return of Christ to manifest itself eucharistically:

> We are here to be transformed: to die to self, live for others, and love like God. That is what's happening on the altar of the earth, just as it happens on the altars of our churches. As the fire descended from heaven to consume the disciples at the first Pentecost. The fire is one and the same; it is the Holy Spirit, Who enables us to be offered up as living sacrifices upon the altar of the earth. That is what makes sense out of the second half of the Apocalypse.[46]

We cannot deny that such an exegesis is both compelling and beautiful, yet, Hahn offers it without any appeal to either patristic, encyclical, or theological sources. It would seem that Hahn is operating more out of the *sola scriptura* exegetical approach of his Calvinist past and, thus, we must be cautious of his conclusion. Despite Hahn's interpretive license here, it is this concluding thought that is the central idea of *The Lamb's Supper*.

More directly, Hahn tells us that the idea behind this book is that Revelation shows us that in the Mass, particularly in the Eucharist, we are quite literally in heaven already. In support of this thesis, he turns to the *Catechism*, "[Worship] participates in the liturgy of heaven," and, "Those who even now celebrate [the liturgy] without signs are already in the heavenly liturgy."[47] While no faithful Catholic theologian can deny that we are participating in the "heavenly liturgy" in the Mass, the *Catechism* qualifies this notion slightly. The first quote that Hahn provides from the *Catechism* is number 1089, but in looking at 1090, which Hahn also provides, we find, "In earthly liturgy we *share in a foretaste* of that heavenly liturgy . . . ."[48]

---

46. Hahn, *The Lamb's Supper*, 136.

47. Hahn, *The Lamb's Supper*, 117. From *The Catechism of the Catholic Church*, nos. 1089 and 1136.

48. Hahn, *The Lamb's Supper*, 117–18. *The Catechism of the Catholic Church*, no.

Hahn unpacks this last notion with a discussion of the Greek word *parousia* (παρουσία). While *parousia* is most often used specifically in regards to the second coming of Christ, Hahn argues that *parousia* primarily refers more broadly to the "real, personal, living, lasting, and active presence [of God]."[49] It is this sense that Hahn employs to read Revelation as indicating that the coming presence of Christ takes place right now in the Mass. As is his custom, Hahn turns to Ratzinger to bolster this conclusion: "liturgy is anticipated Parousia," Ratzinger writes, "the 'already' entering our 'not yet.'"[50]

Here again, the Ratzinger quote does not actually reinforce the idea that Hahn is endorsing, and he provides no other support for his thesis. If we look back to pre-New Testament Greek, we do find the word *parousia* used to mean presence, either in regards to the arrival of a public official or the presence of the gods. In Thucydides's *The Peloponnesian War*, for instance, *parousia* is used to refer to the first time the king had been in a certain city.[51] This meaning of the word is also maintained at times in the New Testament. Second Corinthians 10:10 employs *parousia* to describe Paul's presence in Corinth.[52] In fact, Paul uses this sense of *parousia* far more often than he does for the return of Christ, and when he is referring to the second coming, *parousia* is always joined with some variant of "of Christ" or "of the Lord."

By the end of the New Testament period, however, *parousia* seems to be firmly connected to the return of Christ. In fact, the German theologian Adolf Deismann argued in 1923 that the very idea of Christ's return was intentionally pieced together by the Hellenistic usage of *parousia* denoting the visitation of a king or emperor. This idea was employed by the early Christian community to indicate that Christ will be the final king to arrive, which Deismann cites as further evidence of early Christianity's appropriation of the cult

---

1090, emphasis added.

49. Hahn, *The Lamb's Supper*, 116.

50. Hahn, *The Lamb's Supper*, 116. This quote is originally from Joseph Ratzinger, *A New Song for the Lord*, 129.

51. Thucydides, *The Peloponnesian War*, 2009, 62. Βυζάντιον γάρ ἑλὼν τῇ προτέρᾳ παρουσίᾳ μετὰ τὴν ἐκ Κύπρου ἀναχώρησιν (εἴχοω δὲ Μῆδοι αὐτὸ καὶ βασιλέως προσήκοντές τινες καὶ ζυγγενεῖς οἳ ἑάλωσαν ἐν αὐτῷ) τότε τούτους οὖσ ἔλαβεν ἀποπέμπει βασιλεῖ κρύφα τῶν ἄλλων ζθμμάχων τῷ δὲ λόγῳ ἀπέδρασαν αὐτόν.: "When *he was previously in the area* after his return from Cyprus, he had captured Byzantium, which was then occupied by Persians, including some relatives and members of the King's own family who were taken prisoner in the town," emphasis added.

52. 2 Corinthians 10:10—ὅτι Αἱ ἐπιστολαὶ μέν φησίν βαρεῖαι καὶ ἰσχυραί, ἡ δὲ παρουσία τοῦ σώματος ἀσθενὴς καὶ ὁ λόγος ἐξουθενημένος.: For someone will say, "His letters are severe and forceful, but his bodily presence is weak, and his speech contemptible." (NABRE).

of the emperor for budding christological belief formation.[53] Thus, while the connotation Hahn provides for *parousia* is accurate, employing that meaning in regard to the book of Revelation would appear somewhat anachronistic.

Moreover, it seems unnecessary. The role of the liturgy, as Ratzinger suggested, in bringing the second coming of Christ into the here and now is widely attested to, after a fashion. The French Jesuit Jean Daniélou, in his "Sacraments and Parousia," argues for the sacraments enacting the coming return of Christ for Christians, not in simply a metaphorical sense, but in a fully metaphysical one. Despite this intensely mystical reality taking place in the act of the liturgy, Daniélou is emphatic that the sacraments echo the parousia visible in the sign of the sacrament, but that the reality of the coming return of God, though actual, is hidden from us.[54] This captures the "already, but not yet" hope of the Christian community and mystery of the Mass. So, perhaps Daniélou would disagree with Hahn's depiction of exactly what takes place in the sacraments,[55] but this is not surprising nor should it be viewed as problematic. After all, theologians disagree and discuss and debate. This is just what part of being a theologian. What is problematic is Hahn does not seem to recognize a diversity of theological beliefs and contributions fitting within the confines of the tradition.

Along with Ratzinger, Hahn also references the famed biblical scholar Raymond Brown. In a paper on the Our Father, Brown demonstrates that early Christians were already well aware of the theological connection between the manna of the Exodus story and the Christian communion rite. "And so our Roman Liturgy," Brown concludes, "may not be too far from the original sense of the petition in having the [Our Father] introduce the Communion of the Mass."[56] Relying upon this insight from Brown, Hahn reads the Communion Rite as being built upon the Greek connotation of *communion*, or *koinonia*. Hahn claims that the word *koinonia* was most commonly used in the context of a familial bond and, thus, in the Eucharist, we are renewing our bond with the eternal family of the Trinity.[57]

53. Deissmann, *Light From the Ancient East*, 372.

54. Daniélou, "Sacraments and Parousia," 400.

55 "The Apocalypse shows us that He is here in fullness—in kingship, in judgment, in warfare, in priestly sacrifice, in Body and Blood, Soul and Divinity—whenever Christians celebrate the Eucharist. . . . When Jesus comes at the end of time, He will not have a single drop more glory than He has right now upon the altars and in the tabernacles of our churches." Hahn, *The Lamb's Supper*, 116.

56. Hahn, *The Lamb's Supper.*, 56. While Hahn does not supply the reference, it would appear that Hahn is referencing Raymond Brown, "Pater Noster as Eschatological Prayer." The pertinent quotation appears on p. 199.

57. While this rendering of *koinonia* works for Hahn's discussion, *koinonia* most often appears in terms of voluntary membership in a community and, on rare occasions, as a metaphor for sexual activity.

For Hahn, this renewal of our covenant with the family of the Trinity and the Church in the Eucharist is the moment in which we are "taken up to heaven to join with the heavenly throng in the marriage supper of the Lamb."[58] Moreover, relying upon the previous insight from Brown, Hahn sees this eucharistic insight as having been held just as fully by the New Testament Church and in the teaching of Christ himself. "This is," Hahn contends, "the cold, calculated, precise, metaphysical truth that was taught by Jesus Christ."[59] While it has long been a part of Church teaching that the Eucharist is metaphysical in nature, even perhaps that the writer of John intended to be using strict metaphysical language in regards to the Eucharist, the claim that Jesus Christ understood himself to be speaking in the mode of "cold, calculated, precise" metaphysics at the Last Supper is a claim that just cannot be supported.

Continuing with his discussion, Hahn confesses that it was only once he began participating in the Mass that the pieces of this "puzzling book" began to fall into place. As we have seen, he finds in its apocalyptic imagery an altar, priests, candles, incense, bread, chalices, the Gloria, the Sign of the Cross, and then the constant refrain of the Lamb of God; in short, all the makings of the Mass.[60] According to Hahn, this demonstrates that this Apocalypse of John is not *just* about 1970s geopolitics, first-century Roman history, or instructions for the end times. It is, again, very definitively about the sacrament of the Eucharist.

While he goes on at length about what Revelation depicts through the lens of the Mass, it is this brief examination—just shy of a single page—that Hahn finds sufficient to establish the *key* to the book of Revelation as the Mass. Having concluded the question of Revelation's meaning, he moves on to entertain why such a straightforwardly simple concept, the liturgical celebration of the Eucharist, would have been encoded in such a bizarre presentation. His answer lies in the first-century Jewish and Christian perception of the Temple. Given the centrality of the Temple to Jewish life and worship, Hahn claims that it was crucial for the writer to identify the elements of Temple worship being enacted, not merely by a singular priest entering the Holy of Holies where God resided, but the whole of the heavenly court and a nation of priests participating in an unified, cosmic liturgy.[61] Thus, it is the Jewish Temple of the Old and New Testaments, the Temple envisioned

---

58. Hahn, *The Lamb's Supper*, 57.

59. Hahn, *The Lamb's Supper*, 57.

60. Hahn, *The Lamb's Supper*, 66. Revelation 8:3; 4:4; 1:12; 5:8; 2:17; 16:1–17; 15:3–4; 14:1, respectively.

61. Hahn, *The Lamb's Supper*, 69–70.

in Revelation, and the eucharistic celebration of the Mass that Hahn knits together as the foundation for his discussion.

Hahn confesses that he has not always recognized this connection. He began his examination of Revelation by explaining his past exegetical commitments and their flaws. As a "Protestant, evangelical in expression, Calvinist in theology," Hahn saw the Apocalypse of John as a "puzzle that God dared [him] to crack."[62] This, Hahn argues, is the critical failure of the Protestant reading, of which Hahn appears to recognize only one unified approach, of Revelation. Revelation reveals, he claims, in that it unmasks the prejudices, anxieties, and ideology of each interpreter. It is a "sort of Rorschach blot" in that because it lacks the ordering principles of a literary work it can only act as a mirror of the interpreter. In such cases, as in Hahn's own past approaches, the student of Revelation seizes upon a particular detail that speaks to their underlying assumptions, and that singular piece becomes the interpretive key to the remainder of the Apocalypse. In response to this flawed approach, Hahn suggests that we look to the Church Fathers, "the Christian writers and teachers from the first eight centuries." It is with the Fathers that Hahn finally understood that the Book of Revelation is entirely incomprehensible outside of the context of the liturgy.

Despite the difficulties for Hahn's investigation discussed above, he concludes this section with the claim that the meaning of John's Apocalypse is "often plainly told in the text, or plainly wanting in our hearts."[63] That is, at its core, Revelation is straightforward and intuitive. "You and I," Hahn implores, "need to open our eyes and rediscover this long-lost secret of the Church, the early Christians' key to understanding the mysteries of the Mass, the only true key to the Apocalypse."[64] This characterization is one that, despite Hahn's constant refrain that he is merely echoing tradition, rarely shows up in descriptions of the book of Revelation taken up in the tradition of the Church. The introduction to the book of Revelation from the USCCB's online New Testament presents it as "one of the most difficult [books of the Bible] to understand because it *abounds* in *unfamiliar* and *extravagant symbolism*, which at best appears unusual to the modern reader."[65]

A crucial insight into Hahn's intuitive, exegetical vision of Revelation lies in his treatment of the great final war, Armageddon. While he begins this discussion by referencing biblical futurists of the Hal Lindsey variety, he quickly moves past such important questions concerning the reality of a coming

---

62. Hahn, *The Lamb's Supper*, 62–63.
63. Hahn, *The Lamb's Supper*, 88.
64. Hahn, *The Lamb's Supper*, 128.
65. http://www.usccb.org/bible/scripture.cfm?bk=Revelation&ch=.

cosmic battle by maintaining that if the futurist is correct, a possibility he is willing to entertain, he argues that it cannot be our primary concern.[66] Rather, we must look, he encourages us, to the other senses of Scripture:

> What do we mean by the senses of Scripture? From the earliest times, Christian teachers have spoken of the Bible as having a *literal sense* and a *spiritual sense*. The literal sense may describe a historical person, place, or event. The spiritual sense speaks—*through that same person, place, or event*—to reveal a truth about Jesus Christ, or the moral life, of the destiny of our souls, or all three. Tradition teaches us, however, that the literal sense is foundational. Yet identifying the literal sense of the Book of Revelation is a most difficult enterprise, and it's bound to be controversial. After all, interpreters are sharply divided over whether the book is literally describing past events or future events—or past *and* future events, for the Apocalypse may apply quite concretely to both.[67]

As indicated above, this is an extremely important text for making sense of Hahn's exegetical approach, which is particularly troubling given that there is so much packed into these two paragraphs and very little by way of explanation. First, it must be noted that again, Hahn references tradition teaching us but offers no indication as to *where* he finds this in the tradition, nor does he explain what the writers he is referencing meant by "the literal sense is foundational." In looking at some of his other writings, we able to make better sense of this most critical move.

Hahn, in an introduction to the *Ignatius Study Bible* co-authored with Curtis Mitch,[68] provides the following depiction of the different senses of Scripture. He tells us that, given the Christian belief that the Scriptures have both human and divine authors, we must learn to master two different approaches. First, we must read the Bible in its literal sense, which he goes on to describe as the manner by which "we read any other human literature."[69] This is not to say, he explains, that we must always read the Bible what he calls "literalistically," but rather that we read it "according to the rules that govern its different literary forms of writing, depending on whether we are reading a narrative, a poem, a letter, a parable, or an apocalyptic vision."[70]

---

66. Hahn, *The Lamb's Supper*, 91.

67. Hahn, *The Lamb's Supper*, 91.

68. Curtis Mitch, who has co-authored several works with Hahn, received his MA in theology at the Franciscan University of Steubenville and is a member of and contributor to Hahn's St. Paul Center.

69. Hahn and Mitch, "Introduction to the Ignatius Catholic Study Bible," x.

70. Hahn, *The Lamb's Supper*, 91.

The second sense of Scripture, the spiritual sense, Hahn explains, is what the Holy Spirit is trying to convey through the text, which may be beyond what the human authors have consciously asserted. He goes on to describe three kinds of spiritual senses discussed in the tradition of the Church. The first of these spiritual senses is the allegorical, which is the spiritual and prophetic meaning of biblical history. The allegorical interpretation reveals "how persons, events, and institutions of Scripture can point beyond themselves toward greater mysteries yet to come (OT), or display the fruits of mysteries already revealed (NT)."[71] The second, the typological or moral sense, reveals how the actions of the faithful in the Old Testament and the life of Christ in the New Testament encourage us to form virtuous habits in our own lives. And the final spiritual sense Hahn names the analogical sense. The analogical sense shows how the events recorded in Scripture prefigure our eventual completed deification as well as how the things "seen" on earth are linked to the "unseen" in heaven.

There are a couple of things to note in regards to Hahn's use of the senses of Scripture. First and foremost, the explication of the senses of Scripture given in *The Lamb's Supper* is restricted to two sentences. If this distinction between the literal and spiritual senses is as important as both Hahn and the tradition indicate, then it would seem critical that he would provide a sufficient account of them and then draw those explanations into specific aspects of Revelation. Yet, outside of a brief recognition of the difficulty of interpreting Revelation, Hahn provides very little to guide his audience toward the literal and spiritual senses of the book. Second, the account of the literal and spiritual senses of Scripture, including the three kinds of spiritual senses, that Hahn provides in the Introduction to the *Ignatius Study Bible* is sufficiently different from that which is found, for instance, in *The Catechism of the Catholic Church*.

According to the Catechism, the literal sense is "the meaning conveyed by the words of Scripture and discovered by exegesis," while the spiritual sense is the "realities and events about which [the Bible] speak" functioning as signs. The allegorical sense the *Catechism* describes as recognizing the significance of biblical events as it pertains to either the coming or life of Christ. The moral sense is simply the notion that the events described in Scripture should lead us to act more virtuously. And finally the analogical sense is viewing the realities and events of Scripture in terms of their eternal significance.[72] While the account of the different senses of Scripture

---

71. Hahn, *The Lamb's Supper*, xi.
72. *Catechism of the Catholic Church*, §115–17.

given here in the *Catechism* is straightforward and specific, the rendering provided by Hahn is troublingly vague.

It is this vagueness that allows Hahn to cast the literal sense of Revelation as concerning either past events, future events, or past and future events.[73] Examining John's Apocalypse through the lens of the *Catechism's* account of the literal sense appears to simply mean that we ask what the text itself is trying to convey. An approach that restricts the meaning of apocalyptic literature to only either past or future literal events would be better described as biblical literalism. Importantly, we remember that Hahn begins this discussion by allowing that he does not "rule out the futurist interpretations of Revelation's battles,"[74] a position that has long been a hallmark of traditional biblical literalism.

Moreover, the exegetical approach Hahn offers here differs greatly from the teachings regarding Scripture by the Pontifical Biblical Commission. The Commission's 1993 "The Interpretation of the Bible in the Church," whose preface was written by then Cardinal Joseph Ratzinger, begins with the acknowledgement that the Bible itself bears witness to its own exegetical difficulties. The document references several passages that highlight the complexity of the Scriptures. Chapter 9 of the book of Daniel, for instance, portrays Daniel pondering the meaning of certain prophecies of Jeremiah. The Acts of the Apostles mentions an Ethiopian Christian who similarly struggled with a passage from Isaiah and expressed the need of an interpreter to assist him. Second Peter 1:20 insists that "no prophecy of Scripture is a matter of interpretation" while 3:16 claims that the letters of the apostle Paul contain "some difficult passages, the meaning of which the ignorant and untrained distort, as they do also in the case of the other Scriptures, to their ruin." While recognizing the difficulty of the Scriptures, the document also expresses concern with certain modern approaches like the historical-critical method, as does Hahn, which we will see in the following chapter.

The issue the document takes with the historical-critical method is not necessarily in its approach but in its scope. "For all its overall validity," it states, "the historical-critical method cannot claim to be totally sufficient." This is due to the fact that the method necessarily sets aside aspects of interpretation that are crucial to the text, like inspiration. This is a failing, the document claims, of every exegetical approach and, thus, a truly Catholic exegesis is one that, among other marks, must show a certain pluralism. "No single interpretation can exhaust the meaning of the whole," the document

---

73. Hahn, *The Lamb's Supper*, 92.
74. Hahn, *The Lamb's Supper*, 91.

concludes, "which is a symphony of many voices."[75] In fact, while mentioning concerns with a host of different interpretive approaches, the only model that the document does not find even partially helpful is what it terms the "Fundamentalist Interpretation." The fundamentalist approach, which unduly stresses a literal sense and inerrancy of the text, is dangerous because, by offering a straightforward reading of a text that contains immediate answers to all of life's problems, fundamentalism actually "invites people to a kind of intellectual suicide."[76] Finally, fundamentalism must be rejected as it "injects into life a false certitude, for it unwittingly confuses the divine substance of the biblical message with what are in fact its human limitations."[77] It is precisely this kind of false certitude that Hahn is here suggesting; that there is a *key* to reading Revelation and that by employing it, the Mass, everything becomes clear and accessible to the common interpreter.

This challenge to Hahn's approach is echoed in the Raymond Brown's celebrated *An Introduction to the New Testament*, a book that has become something of a standard of Catholic biblical exegesis. At no point during his discussion of Revelation does Brown offer the Mass as an interpretive key to unpacking the secrets of this obscure biblical text. In fact, Brown offers no single unifying feature of Revelation other than recognizing the book as exemplifying the genre of apocalyptic literature as "the most apocalyptic book in the NT."[78] Rather than searching for a key to unlock the text, Brown simply states that the "symbolism of apocalyptic compels imaginative participation on the part of the hearers/readers."[79] Yale Old Testament scholar John Collins cautions that when engaging apocalyptic biblical passages a "strong theological prejudice" can impede our efforts in understanding a text, and that it is often better to "reserve theological judgment until after we have mastered the literature."[80] While it will be difficult, indeed, to ever consider oneself to have "mastered" a genre, in practice, what Collins offers is that we must always proceed with extreme caution. Despite the recognized difficulties of interpreting Scriptures of any genre, both Brown and Collins provide a second hermeneutical guide. In their discussions, they each model the example put forth by the Pontifical Biblical Commission by providing a survey of different exegetical approaches, discussing the relative strengths and weaknesses of each, and then providing an account that

---

75. The Pontifical Biblical Commission, "The Interpretation of the Bible in the Church."
76. The Pontifical Biblical Commission, "The Interpretation of the Bible in the Church."
77. The Pontifical Biblical Commission, "The Interpretation of the Bible in the Church."
78. Brown, *An Introduction to the New Testament*, 285.
79. Brown, *An Introduction to the New Testament*, 286.
80. Collins, *The Apocalyptic Imagination*, 14.

attempts to synthesize the available insights to the extent possible. Neither seek to step out on definitive interpretations nor concrete applications on their own. For the Pontifical Biblical Commission, Brown, and Collins, caution and careful synthesis of the various wisdom provided by the Christian community is the heart of Catholic exegesis.

Nevertheless, for Hahn, this all builds towards Revelation as a "personal invitation, intended for you and for me from all eternity."[81] The Catholic Mass is founded, however, on the notion that we do not come to faith, belief, or practice in isolation but always already in the context of community. Thomas Merton, in a 1960 article, "Liturgy and Spiritual Personalism," explains that we enter into the liturgy as a community of participants and performers. That is, our invitation is not personal, but rather to the whole of the Church (and through the Church the remainder of humanity) to come together as a "collaboration of free persons" to perform the communal work of the liturgy.[82] It is the catechumen who has responded to the personal invitation into the community of the Church, Merton argues, but the Mass is the resting place of the Christian polis already engaged in the communal work of salvation. To this end, Revelation is not an invitation "for you and for me from all eternity." Rather, it is an invitation for *us* to lose the isolated sense of ourselves in the "salutary self-forgetfulness commanded by Christ" in the work of salvation.[83]

Hahn uses this language of personal invitation to drive his audience toward a choice. Revelation, he proclaims, culminates in a massive battle of which we must all play a part. This is not a battle that stands at the end of time (although, he is willing to countenance the notion that it might also refer to an end-times war), but is fully present throughout the history of the world. It is participation in this war, fighting the literal minions of evil and their strongholds on earth, that allows us to "ascend to heaven" and become that which we are destined to be, "the Bride of the Lamb."[84]

Hahn concludes, "At Mass, we're already in heaven." It is this sentiment, it seems, that allows him to imagine that he is seeing the truth of God in its entirely uninterpreted or, to borrow from Scripture again, that he sees "face to face" rather than "through a glass dimly."[85] The Apocalypse, which Hahn argues would have been read as indicating an "unveiling," teaches the

---

81. Hahn, *The Lamb's Supper*, 127.
82. Merton, "Liturgy and Spiritual Personalism," 496.
83. Merton, "Liturgy and Spiritual Personalism," 496.
84. Hahn, *The Lamb's Supper*, 131.
85. 1 Corinthians 13:12, my paraphrase.

early Church how to worship in that it guides us in the liturgy he finds so present in the John's vision.

There are several issues we need to pause and take note of here. First, the language Hahn employs appears to present the notion that ascension into heaven is dependent upon one's actions in this eternal cosmic battle. It is a deeply traditional Catholic commitment, however, that our salvation is explicitly not founded on personal action. Dietrich von Hildebrand, the twentieth-century German philosopher and theologian, in his *Transformation in Christ*, offers that the "process of being received, embraced, and assumed as it were, which in reference to value as such is present in an analogical sense only, happens actually and literally when we give ourselves to the almighty God who has the power to elevate our being to Himself and to transform it in its very roots."[86] What Hildebrand echoes here is the notion that the action required for our salvation is one of opening and emptying so that God can act within us, judging us according to what our self-emptying, our kenotic acceptance of Christ's sacrifice, allows.

Second, Hahn makes no reference to other Catholic liturgies nor does he present the early Christian Mass as anything significantly different from those of today. He goes on to suggest that the harps and trumpets described in Revelation were simply the organs and pianos of the Mass for that time period, as if any easy switch of the instruments employed in our Sunday Mass for those of theirs provides a straightforward glimpse into first-century liturgy.[87] A simple counterexample to Hahn's flattening out of liturgical diversity in the tradition would be the controversy concerning the liturgical changes invoked in Vatican II's *Sacrosanctum Concilium*. Moreover, while it is critical that the Church maintain a continuity of Catholic worship from the pages of the New Testament to today, it would be bizarre to maintain that the development of, for instance, trinitarian or christological theologies brought about no significant changes to the Mass.

Third, Hahn's constant return to "the Fathers" is significantly problematic in that these "Fathers" are almost entirely unnamed, as are the specific texts from which Hahn is pulling. Even more importantly, he often talks as if these Fathers speak with a unified, singular voice. But a glance at the world of patristic scholarship demonstrates that the first thousand years of the Church were complicated and rich tapestries of flawed believers.[88] Yet,

---

86. Von Hildebrand, *Transformation in Christ*, 232.

87. Hahn, *The Lamb's Supper*, 120.

88. For instance, Justin Martyr and Irenaeus, both first-century Fathers, appear to have taken a much more literal approach to Revelation's depiction of Christ's reign of peace on earth at the end of time, while in the third and fourth centuries, biblical scholars Origen and Jerome, respectively, sharply criticized such literalistic interpretations

despite their flaws, by relying on the grace of Christ through the Church, each strove to rise out of their brokenness and offer guidance and assistance to the Church.[89] To cast the patristic period as an ahistorical unity of thought and belief is to strip it of the very human cost of disagreement, excommunications, and infighting as well as the victories of collaboration, intellectual exchange, and tradition. Moreover, while Hahn at times suggests that certain of his writings fit more easily within the category of "popular" and others as "academic" or "scholarly," an examination of those more scholarly contributions also appear to remain completely silent on the reality of diversity within the Fathers and the tradition at large.

The final troubling aspect of *The Lamb's Supper* is to what the closing sentiments of Hahn lead. According to Hahn, there is a war taking place for which we must choose our sides. On its own, this is a fairly nebulous theological assertion, but Hahn puts it into particular specificity with what follows:

> Yet the power of the saints is of a different order than the world's idea of power, and the wrath of the Lamb differs significantly from human vengeance. That may seem self-evident, but it's worth our deepest contemplation. For many Christians profess to believe in a heavenly sort of power, which, on closer analysis, turns out to be worldly power writ large.[90]

While there is no denying that Christians have, throughout the ages, often mistaken earthly powers for the powers of heaven, Hahn's declaration here is little more than troubling as it stands. Offered without qualification or further explanation, such a statement is yet another instance of a position that allows the speaker to render God's power and action in their own image.

As Hahn himself recognizes, the overwhelming majority of interpreters of Revelation leave with little more than a reflection of their own biases, interests, and exegetical frameworks. It is for Hahn, and those of his methodological approach, that the Apocalypse reveals itself through the work of the Fathers. That is, by looking first to the Church Fathers, Hahn believes that he has, in effect, removed himself from the pages of Revelation. His interpretation is not merely one for which he believes is worth arguing.

---

as introducing myth and fable. Augustine (fourth–fifth century) argued vehemently against every attempt to use the book of Revelation to attempt to identify eschatological specifics. See Koester, "On the Verge of the Millennium."

89. "Patristics has been defined as the study of the writings of the Fathers of the Church; while this definition may still suffice, we might want to ask which Fathers are meant and which Church is being referred to. This is because we are conscious that the early Church was fractured and divided along fault lines that are still visible." Ken Parry, "The Nature and Scope of Patristics," 4.

90. Hahn, *The Lamb's Supper*, 133.

Rather, it is the *only* responsible rendering of the text when one dutifully turns to the wisdom of the Church Fathers.

The Scriptures, however, should not be viewed as a code waiting to be cracked and the attempt to render as simple a book as complex as that of Revelation by claiming to have found the secret cipher buried within, must always be regarded as a mistake. Yet, this is precisely what Hahn does. For example, many of Hahn's conclusions in *The Lamb's Supper* are founded on his attempt to read Jesus as "the Lamb of God" into much of the Old Testament. Going back to Genesis, Abel, Hahn argued, offered a lamb, foreshadowing of Christ's sacrifice to come. Yet, examining the text itself only provides that Abel brought the "fatty portion of the firstlings of his flock."[91] He then goes on to cite from the first-century Jewish historian, Josephus, that shortly before the destruction of the Temple in A.D. 70, the Jewish priests offered an astounding quarter of a million lambs as a sacrifice to God. An investigation of the text from Josephus, however, leaves the specific kind of the animals being sacrificed ambiguous, referring only to "victims."[92] Of course, Catholicism must maintain the presence of eucharistic themes in the Old Testament, yet, his liturgical reading of Revelation has colored his examination of the Hebrew texts and histories.

The aspect of this discussion that we should find particularly troubling is what Hahn offers next:

> I want to make clear that this idea—the idea behind this book— is nothing new, and it's certainly not mine. It's as old as the Church, and the Church has never let go of it, though the idea has been lost in the shuffle of doctrinal controversies over the last several centuries.[93]

His interpretation of the Scriptures and Church tradition is interesting and compelling for a significant number of people. It is, however, *his*. It is shaped by his perspective, personal and intellectual history, walk of faith, and place in life. To borrow from Scripture, Hahn has worked out his faith, and continues to work out his faith, "with fear and trembling."[94]

An interviewer of Jacques Derrida once exclaimed to him in an exasperated tone, "To read you one has to have read Derrida!" to which Derrida

---

91. Hahn, *The Lamb's Supper*, 22. Genesis 4:4. In reading the text, we are actually given surprisingly little. Along with not being told what Abel sacrificed, neither are we told what Cain brought as an offering nor why his was rejected.

92. He writes that "the victims were counted and amounted to 255,600." Josephus, *The Jewish War*, 499.

93. Hahn, *The Lamb's Supper*, 116.

94. Philippians 2:12.

replied simply, "But that's true for everyone."[95] What Derrida was attempting to convey to his interviewer is that there are no texts that stand completely on their own. Every work has a lineage and a story. And to the extent that the Derrida of this 1994 interview is substantially changed from that of the 1974 author of his celebrated *Of Grammatoloy*, the story of his later contributions include an obligation for Derrida to reexamine his own story. That is, we could imagine the interviewer following up with a reminder to Derrida, "To write you have to have read you," to which he would have again responded, "But that's true for everyone."

In *The Lamb's Supper*, Hahn betrays that in his writing he has failed to read himself. That is, he fails to recognize that he brings to his own pages the story of the many movements, victories, and defeats of his life. His repeated assurances that he offers nothing new nor anything that could be properly described as *his* demonstrates Hahn's mistaken belief that he can simply substitute another's story for his own. As we all know all too well, we cannot ever fully escape our past. Our wounds may heal, but the scars, no matter how faint, always remain. Hahn is not the same "Protestant, evangelical in expression, Calvinist in theology" graduate student who began his academic journey so many years ago, yet that does not mean that he is not the same person who lived through it. It is for this reason that we see a constant return to the Scripture only, devoid of any substantial appeal to the tradition. And it is for this reason that he imagines himself to have found the "key"[96] to Revelation, but he cannot recognize himself as continuing to view Revelation as "a puzzle that God dared [him] to crack."[97]

The Lamb's Supper has a story. Hahn has a story. Revelation and its author have a story. The Catholic tradition is a massive web of the stories of the faithful, at times working together with each other and at others pulling against each other across the ages. It is through this storied tradition that we, who each have our own complex and complicated story, are allowed to step into their pages and discover that their story was always already a part of our own.

---

95. Derrida, "Unsealing (the Old New Language)," 117.
96. Hahn, *The Lamb's Supper*, 4.
97. Hahn, *The Lamb's Supper*, 4.

3

Benedict the Inerrantist?

IN 1845, THEN ANGLICAN theologian John Henry Newman published the first edition of his *An Essay on the Development of Christian Doctrine*. His theological contributions having become increasingly critical of the Anglican Church, Newman found himself somewhat adrift without a theological home. Casting about for something to provide him footing, Newman turned to history. Looking to the story of the faith throughout the ages, Newman discovered that the history of Christianity provided what he was looking for:

> Christianity being one, all its doctrines are necessarily developments of one, and if so, are of a necessity consistent with each other, or form a whole. Now the world fully enters into this view of those well-known developments which claim the name of Catholic. It allows them that title, it considers them to belong to one family, and refers them to one theological system.[1]

What Newman so desperately wanted was to find the heart of Christianity, what he refers to as the Idea of Christianity, waiting for him in the present.

Newman believed that there are those ideas whose contents are of such a kind as to act within the mind as a living thing. To this extent, the idea seems to take on its own agency and push the mind into action to either accommodate and nourish it or to fight against it. Yet, what acts as a metaphor with most ideas, according to Newman, becomes a reality in the revelation

---

1. Newman, *An Essay on the Development of Christian Doctrine*, 96.

of God. This Idea of Christianity is God-breathed, and thus it is itself both a communicative and a creative act, sustained and nurtured by the Holy Spirit. Moreover, the Idea of Christianity is passed throughout the centuries ready to be picked up and carried on by the believers of today.

What remains unanswered in Newman, however, is the question of whether or not this development of doctrine that he names the Idea of Christianity actually changes as it evolves throughout the ages. It is this very question that is picked up by John O'Malley in his 2019 article, "Does Church Teaching Change?" in the Catholic publication *Commonweal*.[2] Here, O'Malley addresses the question of doctrinal change through the developments of the council of Trent, Vatican I, and Vatican II. During the Reformation, Luther and his compatriots called for something akin to what in the twentieth century came to be known as *ressourcement*, a return to the sources. What had poisoned fifteenth- and sixteenth-century Catholicism, in the minds of the Reformers, was that the Church had forgotten the Gospels. Luther's "return to the sources" of the Gospels came, O'Malley writes, in the form of his doctrine of justification by faith alone. It was in response to the Protestant challenge at Trent that the Church first formulated the doctrine that would later be christened by the philosopher R. G. Collingwood as substantialism.[3] The sixteenth-century doctrine of the Catholic Church, the Catholic leaders at Trent determined, was simply the Spirit-led continuity of the Gospels' message and, thus, orthodox and true to the tradition.

While the Church reinforced the notion that doctrine did not change at Trent, they did recognize that aspects of the Church did. The Europe of the Reformation had become an incredibly dysfunctional place, and included in that were certain aspects of the Catholic communion. In this regard, despite the doctrine of the Church remaining unchanged, the Church and the faithful, in regards to the world's and even their own wickedness, had to evolve and that became the hallmark of the Catholic conclusion to Trent. To that end, the Church did change certain aspects of its moral teachings. O'Malley offers as an example an added requirement of a priest being witness to a marriage for it to be considered valid, in order to respond to the immorality that had gripped the Western world.[4]

---

2. O'Malley, "Does Church Teaching Change?" John O'Malley is the University Professor of Theology at Georgetown University and a Jesuit priest.

3. O'Malley, "Does Church Teaching Change?"

4. O'Malley, "Does Church Teaching Change?" The Catholic teaching regarding marriage has always been that it is a sacrament in which the participants of the marriage are each solely responsible for the giving of the sacrament to each other. O'Malley demonstrates that the added requirement of the witness of a priest was in response to the rise in the practice of secret marriages, witnessed only by the bride and groom,

The intervening centuries between Trent and Vatican I (1869–70) saw massive shifts in the world of history, philosophy, science, and religion. Not only did the Church witness the development of historical criticism and its employment in scriptural exegetical work,[5] but also the emergence of psychology, religious studies (as a secular discipline), the publication of Darwin's *On the Origin of Species*, and the rise of secular European nation-states. By the time that Pius IX called the First Vatican Council, the question of the Church's response to a quickly changing world became paramount. Vatican I's answer lay in the doctrine of infallibility, which solidified the notion of a continuity of papal teaching throughout the history of the Church. Yet, while it seems that the spirit of Trent's commitment to doctrinal substantialism remained fully enforced in the First Vatican Council's promulgation of papal infallibility, O'Malley demonstrates the crisis of modernism that dominated so much of the Church's attention in the late nineteen and the first half of the twentieth century wrought a definitively different spirit in Vatican II.[6]

Modernism, Pius X's label for the loosely associated commitments to historical criticism, evolution, relativism, humanism, and the like condemned in his 1907 *Pascendi dominici gregis*, launched a period of theological turmoil in the Church that by the Second Vatican Council it, or at least each of its component parts, demanded to be addressed. Yet, if a refusal to admit change defined Vatican I, O'Malley argued, it was the Italian notion of *aggiornamento* that characterized Vatican II. While the notion of changing or updating in response to the cultural climate of the day was certainly at play at both Trent and Vatican I, the *aggiornamento* of the Second Vatican Council (1962–65) was not simply confined to new technologies or social conventions, such as the use of microphones and amplifiers, but rather to "certain cultural assumptions and values" that stemmed directly from previously condemned contributions of Enlightenment thought.[7]

Guiding much of this *aggiornamento* spirit in Vatican II and the period leading up to it, O'Malley writes, was a resurgence of Newman's *An Essay on*

---

which often led to a denial of the marriage by one of the participants in order to abandon, most often, wife and children.

5. For instance, the oft-maligned Jewish philosopher Baruch Spinoza, writing in the seventeenth century, was among the first to apply this new critical approach to historical texts to the Gospels themselves and, subsequently, was ostracized by both Jewish and Christian communities alike.

6. O'Malley, "Does Church Teaching Change?"

7. O'Malley offers "liberty, equality, and fraternity" as the most basic of these assumptions accepted by Vatican II.

the Development of Christian Doctrine.[8] It was in the spirit of Newman that the early twentieth-century's call to *ressourcement*, O'Malley concludes, led to the important notion that a "return to the sources" sometimes demands a recognition that the path taken was the wrong one and nothing but a shift, perhaps what could even be called a change, is the only way forward.

While O'Malley's investigation is excellent and provides a great deal of clarity into a deeply important theological issue, there is one question the article does not answer nor ever even entertain. What was it about the Church and the world of 2019 that led O'Malley to write then, and for *Commonweal* to publish it?

Any investigation into the ideas and work of Scott Hahn would be dramatically incomplete without an examination into the thinkers who have influenced him throughout his formation and career. The most cursory look at any of his writings make it clear that there has been no greater influence on Hahn than the Pope Emeritus, Benedict XVI. In fact, the pope, either under the chosen papal name of Benedict XVI or his given name of Joseph Ratzinger, has appeared in virtually every book that Hahn has written—something that cannot be said of *any* other theologian. Hahn feels so strongly about the central importance of Ratzinger's contributions that he devoted his 2009 *Covenant and Communion* to the investigation of his life and writings. And lest there be any remaining doubt of Hahn's devotion to and admiration of the pope emeritus, the first line of that work reads, "Never before in the history of the Catholic Church has a world class biblical theologian been elevated to the papacy."[9] And indeed, it is Ratzinger's biblical focus that leads Hahn to praise him so highly.

Interestingly, Hahn maintains that it is precisely this biblical nature of Ratzinger's theological contributions that have gone "largely unnoticed in the growing body of secondary literature on Benedict's theological thought and vision."[10] Thus, it is Hahn's hope that through his *Covenant and Communion*, he will bring light to the most central feature of Ratzinger's thought and join with him in offering the faithful a return to a relationship with God founded on the Scriptures. To this end, Hahn describes his intentions here as being to "listen to Benedict, to follow his patterns of thought, and to carefully attend to his priorities and concerns" as well as "to assist in

---

8. O'Malley, "Does Church Teaching Change?"
9. Hahn, *Covenant and Communion*, 13.
10. Hahn, *Covenant and Communion*, 14.

the presentation of Benedict's own ideas, not simply advance [Hahn's] own understanding of these issues."[11]

Our walk through *Covenant and Communion* will need to determine how successful Hahn is in accomplishing what he set out here as his aims; that Ratzinger is the precisely the biblicist that Hahn depicts. In this, it will be crucial that we distill from this work the image of Ratzinger from which Hahn is working. As Hahn is clear that his presentation highlights important central features of Ratzinger's life and work that are largely missing in the remainder of the academy's treatment of him, it is also important that we examine at least a sample of other readings of Ratzinger and determine whether they do in fact overlook the key features to which Hahn alludes. Finally, we must examine some of Ratzinger's own presentations of his thought and determine for ourselves whether his self-assessment agrees with Hahn's depiction.

The now Pope Emeritus Benedict XVI was born at Marktl am Inn, Germany on April 16, 1927 as Joseph Ratzinger. After studying philosophy and theology at the University of Freising, Ratzinger entered the priesthood in 1951. Ratzinger went on to receive his doctorate in theology in 1953 and then qualified for University teaching with a second dissertation in 1957. Having completed the requisite degrees, Ratzinger spent the next, roughly, decade teaching theology at Freising, Bonn, Münster, Tübingen, and then Regensburg, where he also served as vice-president of the university.[12]

Serving as a theological advisor for Cardinal Joseph Frings, archbishop of Cologne, Ratzinger made notable contributions to the Second Vatican Council. In March of 1977, Pope Paul VI named him archbishop of Munich and Freising and then later that same year a cardinal. One of the more significant events in Ratzinger's rise to prominence, however, came in November of 1981 when John Paul II named him prefect of the Congregation for the Doctrine of the Faith. This position of incredible influence on the shape of Catholic doctrine Ratzinger held for more than two decades. After the death of Pope John Paul II in April of 2005, Ratzinger was elected on April 18, 2005 as the 265th pope as Benedict XVI. He served as pope until February 28, 2013 when, citing "the certainty that my strengths, due to an advanced age" had rendered him "no longer suited to an adequate exercise of the Petrine ministry," he became the first pope in the history of the Roman Catholic Church to resign.[13]

---

11. Hahn, *Covenant and Communion*, 16.
12. "Biography of His Holiness, Pope Benedict XVI."
13. Benedict XVI, "Declaratio."

As we noted above, Hahn's interest in Ratzinger's remarkable career is what Ratzinger himself names the "biblical character" of his thought and work.[14] That is, Ratzinger names the Word as "the point of departure" for his theology and, in fact, for all proper theological investigation.[15] "How we read and interpret the Bible," Hahn understands him as arguing, "directly affects what we believe about Christ, the sacraments, and the liturgy."[16] And to this end, it is the recognition of the unity of the Old and New Testaments that stand as the key to understanding Ratzinger's theological approach. Yet, Hahn argues, for Ratzinger it is "the Church alone that makes the disparate texts into a single book, into a Bible."[17] It is this unity through the lens of the Church's practice of faith that most clearly reveals the person of Jesus Christ, the Son of God.

For Ratzinger, Hahn proclaims, the work of the Church's theological inquiries are always directed toward the preaching and teaching of the Church through which the past words and actions of Jesus become "a present reality."[18] In the Church's work of bringing the gospel into the current discourse, Ratzinger turns to St. Bonaventure for some helpful distinctions. As Hahn understands it, Ratzinger recognizes Bonaventure's classifications of *theologìa* (θεολογία) and *theologichē* (θεολογιχή) for theological discourse. *Theologìa*, which literally renders as "the speech of the gods [or god]," Bonaventure reserves for the revelation of the Scriptures.[19] In its most straightforward formulation, Ratzinger returns to Aristotle, who reserved for the gods speaking either themselves or through, for instance, the ancient poets, *theologìa*, and relied upon *theologichē* to describe all human efforts to understand the divine.[20] Hahn recognizes in Ratzinger's discussion an important "elevating and restoring" of theology to its privileged position.[21] In so doing, Ratzinger places at the heart of theology the *theologoi* of the

---

14. Hahn, *Covenant and Communion*, 93.
15. Hahn, *Covenant and Communion*, 92.
16. Hahn, *Covenant and Communion*, 20.
17. Hahn, *Covenant and Communion*, 100.
18. Hahn, *Covenant and Communion*, 55.
19. Hahn, *Covenant and Communion*, 87.
20. Joseph Ratzinger, *Principles of Catholic Theology*, 321. It should be noted here that the distinctions Ratzinger here employs are for the purposes of answering the questions as to whether theology is, most fundamentally, a speculative or practical undertaking. The context in which Hahn entertains Benedict's discussion is aimed at a defense of the Scriptures against what Hahn sees as the abuses of the historical-critical method. While such a move is problematic, I do not address it here as it still serves to present the depiction of Ratzinger with which Hahn is working.
21. Hahn, *Covenant and Communion*, 88.

Scriptures, that is, the living words of God in the mouths of the authors of Scripture, rendering the subject of theology not the abstract idea of God, but rather the vibrant faith of God's self-disclosure.

It is in this privileging of the Scriptures as the *theo-logos*, or the words spoken by God, that Hahn presents Ratzinger's driving concern throughout the entirety of his career as protecting, defending, and constantly returning to sacred Scripture. Such a claim, however, entails that Benedict must have been restoring Scripture from some kind of assault. And it is this attack that provides context for the entirety of Ratzinger's efforts.

Hahn and, by his estimation, Ratzinger, recognize in what has become known as the historical-critical method the most dramatic attack to the truth and accessibility of the Scriptures. The historical-critical method, at its foundation, is "the effort to establish in the field of history a level of methodological precision that would yield conclusions of the same certainty as in the natural sciences."[22] Such a methodology, then, seeks to strip from historical accounts and their transmission throughout history human biases, values, and characteristics. When applied to the Bible, historical criticism looks for more original sources in an attempt to discover the historically "pure" facts of the scriptural events that have been buried under the layers of biased perspective and later theological anachronistic vision.

Hahn is correct in portraying Ratzinger's interest in modern scriptural exegesis as being committed to purification rather than rejection.[23] It cannot be denied that the historical-critical approach has at times deepened our understanding of the people and events of the Scriptures. We understand more about who these people were, how they organized their lives and walks of faith, and most importantly, what they believed. The dream of this modern exegetical approach is, of course, quite compelling, particularly for Christians. Who among us would not want to know Jesus and the apostles more deeply, more purely? To be able to one day see Christ for ourselves, to experience Christ—is that not the very heart of Christian faith and hope?

Yet, as Hahn demonstrates, such hope leads, for Ratzinger, merely to the replacing of one set of biases, the writers and historical interpreters of Scripture, for another, those of the historical-critical exegetes themselves. Moreover, such misguided aims also assume that behind the vision of the New Testament events that we have been given lies some "original, primitive simplicity in the way Christians understood the identity of Jesus."[24] Modern biblical scholarship has not yet, however, offered us any particular

---

22. Ratzinger, "Biblical Interpretation in Crisis," 246.
23. Hahn, *Covenant and Communion*, 27.
24. Hahn, *Covenant and Communion*, 30.

reason to think that such a notion is true other than what Hahn suggests is an inherited Enlightenment unease with robust metaphysical belief systems.

Removing Christian theological biases from the Scriptures does not leave one with a more pure and undefiled scriptural account, but rather with something that is not the Bible at all. For Hahn, Ratzinger's "purified" historical-critical take on the Bible restores to the Scriptures the very historical notion that the Scriptures are God-breathed. For the Christian, it is simply a fact of history that God inspired the authors to write as they did and that God safeguards the revelation of Scripture throughout history. Removing faith from the discussion of the historicity of the Scriptures, then, can only be anti-historical.[25] This is even more critical in regards to the Catholic faith, in that it is a core tenet of the faith that in the contemporary liturgy and preaching, the seemingly "past word and action of Jesus" become "a present reality."[26]

Here lies the thrust of Hahn's account of Ratzinger. For Hahn, that to which Ratzinger's life of work is always in service is the defending of the notion that the proper exegetical approach to the Scriptures is the liturgy. "For Benedict," Hahn writes, "the Church's sacramental liturgy—the new covenant's worship—is the goal and consummation of the biblical story and the history of salvation."[27] Hahn makes it clear that, even in this privileging of the liturgy, Ratzinger continues to draw upon the historical study of religion.[28] For Ratzinger, faith and reason must be always working together. To this end, Ratzinger is clear that "exegetes and theologians must be people of faith, men and women seeking to understand the mystery they have given their lives to in the Church."[29] In Hahn's account, Ratzinger's central concern is the protection of the Scriptures, the "elevating and restoring" of the Scriptures to their rightful place, against the attacks of those who do not attend to the Scriptures *faithfully*,[30] a claim that naturally leads us to ask what faithful attending to the Scriptures looks like.

The faithful interpretation of Scripture is somewhat difficult to distill from Hahn's comments here, but he provides us some hints along the way. First, in returning to his discussion of historical-critical approaches, he describes Ratzinger as questioning this methodology by borrowing from science. We have proven that scientific research has been found at times to be

---

25. Hahn, *Covenant and Communion*, 44.
26. Hahn, *Covenant and Communion*, 55.
27. Hahn, *Covenant and Communion*, 166.
28. Hahn, *Covenant and Communion*, 154
29. Hahn, *Covenant and Communion*, 188.
30. Hahn, *Covenant and Communion*, 88.

affected by the actual observation of researchers and certain outcomes compromised by the presuppositions of interpreters. The same occurs, Ratzinger contends, in historical-critical examinations of Scripture.[31] Hahn proceeds to identify the assumptions he, and presumably Ratzinger, see at work in modern approaches. Yet, Hahn never returns to this question in recognition that, no matter the approach, the act of reading itself necessitates some intervention into a text. As we discussed previously, we cannot but read a text through the lens of our experience, education, and perspective. And this omission provides us with our first brick in the foundation of Hahn's Ratzinger on Scripture. There is no faithful *interpretation of* Scripture, only faithful *attention to* Scripture in which the human element is absent.

This first attribute of a Ratzingerian approach is reinforced by the second. Hahn, in critiquing the evolutionary assumptions of historical criticism, mourns the loss of the "plain sense" of Scripture.[32] That is, he contends that in peeling back the layers of a text's formation we become somewhat blinded by later developments of Catholic doctrine anachronistically read into a fundamentally less sophisticated biblical text, and thus lose its original meaning. The removal of the human element in attending to Scripture thus results in the vindication of the plain sense of Scripture, which is available to all who read Scripture from the context of faith. Hahn goes on to clarify this notion of a plain sense by contrasting it against scholarship. "Biblical scholarship," Hahn concludes, "denies in principle that we can know anything with certainty about whether God acts or causes anything to happen in the world."[33] The merits of such an argument notwithstanding, what interests us here is the opposition of the plain sense of the biblical text on the one hand with the fruits of "biblical scholarship" on the other.

The third foundational piece of Hahn's Ratzinger on the Bible is, as mentioned above, a hermeneutic of faith. He reads Ratzinger as suggesting, I would argue rightly, that any attempt at interpretation is doomed to fail if not born of a context of faithful Christian practice from within the community of the Church. What this life of faith offers, however, is access to this plain sense of the biblical text. Hahn supports this claim by citing

---

31. Hahn, *Covenant and Communion*, 28

32. Hahn, *Covenant and Communion*, 32.

33. Hahn, *Covenant and Communion*, 33. It should be noted that Hahn here is discussing the postulate of objectivity in the natural sciences applied to biblical exegesis. This postulate of objectivity questions humanity's epistemological access to certainty regarding causes of natural events. That is, given the position of ourselves within the natural world, we are always already subject to the natural causes of the world, and thus, so are our investigations of it, and we are therefore incapable of climbing out of our position in the world to achieve some entirely unbiased analysis of it.

Ratzinger's assertion that "[faith] has a contribution to make with regard to the interpretation of Scripture."[34] This cornerstone of accessing Scripture leads Hahn to characterize Ratzinger's body of theological work in a very peculiar fashion.

The keystone of Hahn's Ratzinger on Scripture is that, given that faithful attention to the Scriptures demands a context of faith, Ratzinger's approach is not a system:

> The "hermeneutic of faith" proposed by Benedict is less an interpretive "system" than it is a spiritual disposition toward the study of the sacred page; . . . it is perhaps best described as a kind of loving and reverent *listening*, a seeking after the voice of God who in his gracious love speaks to man in the human words of the biblical texts.[35]

This depiction of Hahn's approach as "less of a system" is sharpened just a single page later with the claim that "Benedict does not propose a theological system."[36] Rather, it is a listening informed by a life of faith, through participation in the liturgy.

Before moving on, we need to make sure we are clear as to what Hahn offers in Ratzinger's commitment to "faithful attention" to the Scriptures. First, it is not an interpretation, in that it is free of the biases of modern exegetes. Second, it is a simple looking for the plain sense of the Scriptures. Third, this plain sense is discovered only within the confines of Christian faithfulness and as such, fourth, it is a listening to Scripture rather than the imposition of a theological system. What remains unclear, at least for the moment, is what Hahn believes to be the fruit of such an approach. Before we turn to that question, however, we need to investigate whether this depiction of Ratzinger accords or differs from the remainder of the academy.

It is important that we make clear exactly that for which we are looking. Hahn's Ratzinger is, first and foremost, biblical. The entirety of Ratzinger's theology is committed to the explication and defense of the Scriptures. Second, his concern is largely with the abuses of the historical-critical examination of the Bible. And lastly, Hahn's Ratzinger represents the first time in the history of the Church that "a world class biblical theologian been elevated

---

34. Hahn, *Covenant and Communion*, 45. This quotation comes from Ratzinger, "Relationship between Magisterium and Exegetes." Address to the Pontifical Biblical Commission."

35. Hahn, *Covenant and Communion*, 45, emphasis added. It is critical to note that Hahn goes on to describe this listening, for Ratzinger, as one assisted by the "critical tools of modern exegetical science along with ancient interpretive methods and perspectives." It is not clear, however, as to how Hahn believes these tools should be employed.

36. Hahn, *Covenant and Communion*, 46.

to the papacy."[37] That is, by Hahn's estimation, Ratzinger stands uniquely as a turning point in a return to the Scriptures and a defense of the truth of Christianity. We will be looking for this Ratzinger, particularly insofar as he offers anything resembling Hahn's "plain sense," in the works of other prominent theologians as we move forward.

To aid us in the examination we will be looking at the contributions of Cyril O'Regan, Tracey Rowland, Lieven Boeve, Edward Oakes, Tom Gourlay, and Gerard Mannion and their different assessments of Ratzinger's project.

RATZINGER AND AUGUSTINE

While Hahn describes Ratzinger as a fundamentally *biblical* theologian, many scholars have taken note of the prominent role Augustine plays in Ratzinger's work. In fact, in 1953 his first of the two doctoral dissertations required to teach in the German university system was an explication and celebration of Augustine's doctrine of the Church. Over half a century later, he published as Pope Benedict XVI in 2008, *Church Fathers: From Clement of Rome to Augustine*, in which he examined the lives and works of key figures from the first several centuries of the Church. Most notably, for our purposes, not a single analysis in the book requires more than two sections of exploration except that of Augustine, who apparently merited five. While this could simply be a function of Augustine's substantial bibliography, Ratzinger helps us by crystallizing his feelings thus, "I feel [Augustine] is like a man of today, a friend, a contemporary who speaks to me, who speaks to us with his fresh and timely faith."[38]

Ratzinger does not just begin and end his career with investigations of Augustine, the remainder of his decades of work demonstrates a definitively Augustinian style. For both O'Regan and Rowland, the manner by which Ratzinger discusses the necessary connection between faith and reason, particularly in his essay "What Keeps the World Together," offers that faith and reason, when not properly wedded to each other and both emboldened and restrained by each other, beget violence.[39] Faith, without the guiding hand of reason, leads to fanaticism. And reason, when deprived of the influence of faith, renders the whole of reality as stripped of mystery and beauty, only something that waits to be conquered. This is a theme that, according

---

37. Hahn, *Covenant and Communion*, 13.

38. O'Regan, "Benedict the Augustinian," 24. As O'Regan only provides a portion of the line here, the full quotation is taken from Benedict XVI, *Church Fathers: From Clement to Augustine*, 178.

39. Rowland, "The World in the Theology of Joseph Ratzinger/Benedict XVI," 109–10.

to O'Regan, Ratzinger gleaned from Augustine in his *City of God*, in which the properly ordered Christian life and society offers peace and complementarity as its hallmark.[40]

RATZINGER AND RETREAT FROM THE WORLD

The theological community has also identified an Augustinian rejection of the secular world in Ratzinger's work. While Augustine and Ratzinger both describe the Catholic Church of their periods as suffering through crises of anti-Christian attack, for many commentators, Ratzinger's sharp rejection of modern secularism is so central that it is seen as the defining theme of his contributions. It cannot be denied, of course, that Ratzinger is concerned with a host of theological and epistemological issues, yet Boeve, for instance, argues that what they all point towards is Ratzinger's conviction that there has been an utter breakdown in the foundations of modern thinking.[41] According to this depiction of Ratzinger, the crisis of modernity has forced the Church to address two fundamental questions of the Christian worldview. First, what is Christian truth and how has it developed throughout history? Second, what is the Church's role in teaching that truth?

In looking at Ratzinger through the lens of the Church and the world, it is clear that his career is marked by an evolution in the Catholic response to each of these questions. Despite what appears to be two distinct periods of thought in this regard, the first during his work as a theologian and then second as prefect for the Congregation for the Doctrine of the Faith, Ratzinger's underlying answer to these questions has remained constant. What does change for Ratzinger is his conviction, following the Second Vatican Council, that much of Catholicism had sold out to the allure of modernity.[42] During the period leading up to the council Ratzinger described himself as being somewhat more open to the notion of Church reform, yet upon seeing how some were implementing the determinations of Vatican II, Ratzinger became concerned particularly with the degree to which some theologians were willing to countenance a harmonious alliance with the world.[43]

While Ratzinger was at one time more willing to entertain notions of reform and nonconfrontation, to Hahn's point, his theological concerns have always centered on the interplay of Scripture and tradition. Rather than characterizing Ratzinger as a straightforward biblical exegete, Boeve's

40. O'Regan, "Benedict the Augustinian," 39–41.
41. Boeve, "Introduction," 7.
42. Boeve, "Introduction," 12.
43. Boeve, "Introduction," 12.

treatment of Ratzinger emphasizes his commitment to the notion that God's revelation, while principle and certain through the Scriptures, continues on throughout the tradition of the Church even until today. Such a sentiment is clearly seen in his book published with Karl Barth in 1965, *Revelation and Tradition*, in which they argue that Scripture and tradition must always be seen as two aspects of the much larger story of the revelation of God to humanity.[44] In this regard, characterizing Ratzinger simply as a biblical theologian would be to disregard his conviction that revelation does not reside in the Scriptures by themselves, but rather in the Scriptures read, heard, and shaped into the continued life of faith in the Church.[45] Thus, Ratzinger was certainly concerned about efforts to render Scripture as compatible with the assumptions of modernity, but this worry was always in regards to the danger of the entirety of the faith being manipulated into something fully reconcilable with modern secularism.[46] And this is what Ratzinger was convinced would lead to the utter downfall of Christianity.

RATZINGER AND RELATIVISM

For some interpreters of Ratzinger, the complementarity of faith and reason as an act of defiance against modernity stops just short of the core of Ratzinger's theological concern. According to this perspective, Ratzinger was most concerned about the disastrous effects wrought by the division of faith and reason, crystallized in the fool's hope of early twentieth-century logical positivism. Gourlay, for instance, argues that Ratzinger's primary concern was the way in which the positivistic impulses of the modern world reduce truth to function and the quest for knowledge to the mere maximizing of utility.[47] In short, it is difficult to read Ratzinger without recognizing the importance he places on the grip of relativism on the modern world. "We are moving toward a dictatorship of relativism," Ratzinger laments, "which does not recognize anything as certain and which has as its highest goal one's own ego and one's own desires."[48]

Oakes sheds some light on Ratzinger's obsession with the looming relativist threat by demonstrating that, rather than retreat, his theology has always taken on relativism directly. The relativist intuition always falters,

---

44. Boeve, "Introduction," 13–14.

45. Barth and Ratzinger, *Revelation and Tradition*, 35–37.

46. Boeve, "Theological Foundation: Revelation, Tradition, and Hermeneutics," 28.

47. Gourlay, "The Nuptial Character of the Relationship between Faith and Reason in the Thought of Joseph Ratzinger/Benedict XVI," 267.

48. Ratzinger, "Homily at the Mass for the Election of the Roman Ponitff," 22.

Ratzinger proves, in the face of the horrors of child molestation, female circumcision, suttee, and the like. Ratzinger did not devote his efforts to the warning against relativism, then, but rather "in his steady way, and over the course of a scholarly career spanning half a century, *resolved* the many paradoxes of relativism . . . ."[49] Ratzinger resolves these many paradoxes in the only manner possible, by appealing to Christology.

Relativism was given one of its most theologically definitive forms in Ratzinger's day in the Christological relativism of Ernst Troeltsch. Christian tradition holds that Christ's saving work stands at the center of the entirety of history, yet Troeltsch, relying on the contributions of historical-critical method, concluded that religion, in which he also included Christianity, must be recognized as always historically and geographically located. That is, those Christian claims concerning the centrality of Christ can only have a referent and a meaning from within the Christian tradition and community and, thus, none outside of it.

While the reach of the relativist critique of the traditional self-understanding of Christianity is vast, defending against its assault on Christology must be the Church's first impulse and, indeed, where Ratzinger begins. He maintains that a proper employment of historical-criticism when applied to the historical fact of the person of Jesus Christ unearths truth that requires the rejection of the types of limitations employed by Troeltsch and his ilk. Historical-criticism generates a depiction of Christ that is introductory rather than final.[50] This method allows us to see more clearly the import of Christ's life and teachings from within his locatedness, yet forces us to recognize that, in the scope of his assertions, Christ intends to transcend time and place. Yet again, however, Ratzinger tells us that to answer the claims of Christ that historical-criticism refines for us, we must step beyond the borders of the method and entertain the notion that in Christ, God stepped into history.

For these interpreters, like Gourlay and Oakes, Ratzinger's most central contribution lies in his insistence that relativism fails in the face of Christ. That is, the historical examination of the life of Christ demonstrates that the question of salvation appears in every time and every place and, further, that Christ either definitively and objectively answers that question or does not. While they recognize other facets of Ratzinger's engagement with relativism—for instance, his critique of Marxism, the not unrelated rejection (at least in part) of liberation theology, etc.—they conclude it is the christological victory over the relativist impulse that both unites his work and demonstrates his genius.

49. Oakes, S.J., "Resolving the Relativity Paradox," 93.
50. Oakes, S.J., "Resolving the Relativity Paradox," 104.

RATZINGER AND LITURGY

For still others, Ratzinger does indeed hold out the marriage of faith and modernity (and then postmodernity) as the great poison of the contemporary Church, yet rather than theological insight, it is first and foremost the *liturgy* that is its antidote.[51] For Ratzinger, the liturgy does not make sense of the Scriptures and the Scriptures then the liturgy, but rather the liturgy makes sense of the Church and the Church makes sense of the liturgy.

The way that such a notion plays out is in his conviction that the Church is, first and foremost, a liturgical community. Mannion argues that for Ratzinger, in the fight to advance the Church and its faith, we are not jointly offering the Scriptures and an external society of believers founded on them, but rather the celebration of the Eucharist as the location of the intersection of the practice of faith and the redemptive love of Christ, historically situated in the Scriptures but neither restricted to them nor limited by them.[52] The notion of biblical theology itself would appear to be at odds with, at least as Mannion depicts it, the interlocking nature of Ratzinger's faith, which unites Scripture, tradition, and liturgy to such a degree that there can be no clear lines of demarcation between one and the others. All three are irrevocably bound together for Ratzinger in their "common witness to the revelation of God."[53]

We must allow that there are many theologians who argue that this simple unity of the triad of faith Ratzinger offers is at times infected with a rhetorical and dialectical nostalgia for incomplete or imagined tradition, Scripture, and moral narratives.[54] The merits of such critiques notwithstanding, it is this unity of Scripture, tradition, and liturgy under the umbrella of revelation to which those like Mannion read Ratzinger as committing his efforts.

A catalogue of scholarly approaches to Ratzinger's career could go on almost *ad infinitum*, but for the sake of brevity, the above is sufficient to determine that there is much disagreement in terms of how to view his work.[55]

---

51. Mannion, "Liturgy, Catechesis, and Evangelization," 225.
52. Mannion, "Liturgy, Catechesis, and Evangelization," 228.
53. Mannion, "Liturgy, Catechesis, and Evangelization," 230.
54. Mannion, "Liturgy, Catechesis, and Evangelization," 241.

55. The wide spectrum of depictions of Ratzinger and his theological project is only to be expected given the both the duration of his theological work as well as the variety of responsibilities he was given throughout his long career. While there are those who try to provide some sort of consistent thread to his theological interests, as demonstrated above, very few scholars would be willing to suggest that such threads indicate a singular theological concern rather than an apparent logic (one among many) to the web of theological interests that have guided Ratzinger throughout his career.

Regardless, however, the theme, time and again, is that Ratzinger has been most concerned with some aspect of the response of Christian faith and tradition to contemporary society. While the Scriptures have played a very prominent role in Ratzinger's contributions, the notion that this renders him in some way a "biblical theologian," as Hahn portrays him, misunderstands the very Catholic notion that the current work of the Church is always in the mode of continuing, broadening, and explicating the scriptural foundations of Catholic faith. Not only is this a distinction that Ratzinger never reserves for himself, but surely to the extent that Catholic theology is not in some way biblical, it cannot be truly Catholic.[56] That such work is not always overtly biblical exegesis cannot be allowed in any way to disqualify or impugn it. Moreover, the difference between the above discussions and that offered by Hahn is that Hahn alone describes his approach to Ratzinger in terms of wanting "to listen to Benedict, to follow his patterns of thought, and to carefully attend to his priorities and concerns," implying that this is not the approach of other interpreters of Ratzinger.[57] In explaining the failure of others in not labelling Ratzinger a biblical theologian, Hahn argues not that he disagrees with the conclusions of other scholars, but that "the facts" he identifies "have gone largely unnoticed in the growing body of secondary literature."[58]

Despite the imposition of a traditionally more Evangelical classification of Ratzinger's work in the face of the scholarly community overwhelmingly resisting such an interpretation, there are other significant issues with Hahn's interpretation of Ratzinger's contributions. First, while Hahn is correct that Ratzinger has spoken often and strongly on the perils of the historical-critical method, the manner in which he depicts Ratzinger's role in the story of historical-criticism fails to include the context by which Ratzinger inherited such a perspective. In many ways, it was Pope Leo XIII's 1879 *Aeterni Patris* that began the Catholic pushback against the promises modernity offered to Catholic theology. Emerging from a crisis of modern approaches rebuking traditional Thomism, *Aeterni Patris* called for a hermeneutic of suspicion in regards to an overemphasis on modern approaches to the Scriptures, even while cautiously praising their ingenuity. Leo writes:

---

56. The closest Ratzinger ever comes to describing himself in a manner akin to Hahn's "Biblical theologian" is in his recognition that he considers himself a theologian "directly addressed by the bible today." See Ratzinger, *Jesus of Nazareth: From the Baptism in the Jordan*, Vol. 1.

57. Hahn, *Covenant and Communion*, 15.

58. Hahn, *Covenant and Communion*, 14.

> Therefore, Divine Providence itself requires that in calling back the people to the paths of faith and salvation, advantage should be taken of *human science* also, an approved and wise practice which history testifies was observed by the most illustrious Fathers of the Church. They, indeed, were wont neither to belittle nor undervalue the part that reason had to play. . . .
>
> We know that there are some who, in their overestimate of the human faculties, maintain that as soon as man's intellect becomes subject to divine authority it falls from its native dignity, and hampered by the yoke of this species of slavery, is much retarded and hindered in its progress toward the supreme truth and excellence. *Such an idea is most false and deceptive, and its sole tendency is to introduce foolish and ungrateful men willingly to repudiate the most sublime of truths, and reject the gift of faith, from which the foundations of all good things flow out upon civil society.*[59]

While what Leo cautions here is directed toward historical-criticism in its infancy and even then only implicitly, the discussion begun in *Aeterni patris* is brought to more outright condemnation under Pope Pius X's 1907 *Pascendi dominici gregis*. Explicitly directed toward those the Church labelled "modernists," in reality a very loose association of scholars for which historical-critical methodology was one identifying mark, *Pascendi* accuses the modernists of splitting history into the categories of so-called "real" on the one hand and "faith" on the other. These separate categories of real and faith both offered very different Christs, something the Church steadfastly refused to accept, and, thus, began the formal Catholic rejection of the search for the historical Jesus:

> For the modernists distinguish very carefully between these two kinds of history, and it is to be noted that they oppose the history of faith to real history precisely as real. Thus we have a double Christ: a real Christ, and a Christ, the one of faith, who never really existed; a Christ who has lived at a given time and in a given place, and a Christ who has never lived outside the pious meditations of the believer—the Christ, for instance, who we find in the Gospel of St. John, which is pure contemplation from beginning to end.[60]

This call to arms of *Pascendi*, promulgated in September 1907, as well as of his months earlier *Lamentabili sane*, the "Syllabus Condemning the

---

59. Leo XIII, *Aeterni Patris*, §3, 9. Emphasis added.
60. Pius X, *Pascendi dominici gregis*, §31.

Errors of the Modernists," brought the Catholic condemnation of historical-criticism to a climax. In an effort to quell what they saw as a dangerous doctrinal uprising, the Church added the works of many so-called modernists to *The Index*, a list of books banned for Catholics, and removed many of them from teaching positions at Catholic universities. By the time that Ratzinger began his academic career, the modernists had been almost entirely stamped out by ecclesial authority, and Catholic theologians who shared any historical critical sympathies were strongly rebuked. For instance, the great Jesuit *ressourcement* theologian Henri de Lubac was banned from teaching theology for his perceived modernist sympathies until the somewhat qualified victory of historical-criticism in Vatican II.

The manner by which Hahn portrays Ratzinger's role in the fight against the abuses of historical-criticism, however, make it appear as if Ratzinger's critique of that methodology as well as his call to return to more orthodox scriptural exegesis were the result of his ingenuity alone. For instance, Hahn's presentation of Ratzinger responding to the French modernist Alfred Loisy (1857–1940) completely overlooks the fact that by the time of Ratzinger's rejection of his work in 1977, Loisy's commitments left him laicized and excommunicated from the Church in 1908.[61] To this end, Ratzinger cannot be presented as almost singularly turning the tide against historical-criticism and then later relativism (another alleged hallmark of the modernists), as his notable and praiseworthy work was in line with almost a century-long tradition of the Church's condemnation of both.

Second, while the response to these concerns might point to the fact that Hahn's discussion in *Covenant and Communion* is explicitly oriented towards Ratzinger's theological contribution, such oversight leaves Hahn free to apply Ratzinger's conclusions to areas to which he does not commit himself. In his concluding chapter, for instance, Hahn recounts Ratzinger's analysis of the hostility that existed between Jesus and the perceived Scripture experts of his day. Here, Hahn offers, "It is hard not to hear a contemporary application in Benedict's reading of Jesus' experience."[62] He follows this with a retelling of a story that Ratzinger returns to quite frequently in his work, in which Vladimir Soloviev depicts the Antichrist as a "renowned exegete, so highly regarded that he is awarded an honorary degree in theology from the University of Tübingen."[63] This story, for Ratzinger, serves as a warning about the potential destructiveness of misguided and unreflective scholarly exegesis. Hahn here, however, employs the language of "ally of the

---

61. Hahn, *Covenant and Communion*, 125.
62. Hahn, *Covenant and Communion*, 188.
63. Hahn, *Covenant and Communion*, 189.

enemy" to invoke the notion that Ratzinger divides the scholarly landscape in this regard between good and evil.

The problem with Hahn's presentation here is that Ratzinger had just as much an opportunity as Hahn to apply Jesus' experience with the religious experts of his time to the current world of Catholic theology and yet, Ratzinger did not. He does not conclude, as Hahn does, that Soloviev's story of the Antichrist is a confession that he, too, sees the battle for proper scriptural exegesis as one between God and "the enemy." Rather, it would seem that the theologian that Ratzinger most wants to warn is, in fact, another "famous exegete" with ties to "Tübingen," himself, and only then after that self-directed caution the remainder of the Catholic academy. The proper historical context for Ratzinger's work allows us to recognize that rather than seeing himself as a singular voice standing virtually alone against a wave of modern and postmodern liberalism, Ratzinger's faith situates himself firmly within the tradition, with confidence that the work of Catholic theology, bolstered by millennia of Christian faithfulness, is ever and always drawing the testimony of the Scriptures into the modern world in crucial and compelling ways.

There is one last concern with Hahn's depiction of Ratzinger, but for the moment we will move on to the question of why Hahn attempts to present Ratzinger in this fashion. The reason that Hahn and his compatriots make such a move lies in their attempt to render Ratzinger as endorsing what lies at the heart of Hahn and the St. Paul Center: biblical inerrancy.

In 2010, Hahn and the St. Paul Center devoted an entire volume of the Center's scholarly journal, *Letter & Spirit*, of which Hahn is the editor, to the mysteries and "mission of the incarnate Word."[64] The author (we are never given a name) of the introduction to this volume goes on to describe this *mystery* as something that "theologians have traditionally considered . . . under the heading of the *inspiration and truth* of sacred Scripture or, to use a slightly older nomenclature, *the inspiration and inerrancy* of Scripture."[65] As justification for using the term "inerrancy," they offer the following from Pius XII's 1943 *Divino afflante spiritu*:

> For as the substantial Word of God became like human beings in all things "except sin," so the words of God, expressed in human language, are made like to human speech in every respect *except error*. In this consists that "condescension" of the God of

---

64. Hahn, "Introduction," 14.
65. Hahn, "Introduction," 14.

providence, which St. John Chrysostom extolled with the highest praise and repeatedly declared to be found in the sacred books.[66]

Following in this encyclical tradition, Hahn, in his essay "For the Sake of Our Salvation: The Truth and Humility of God's Word," defends the notion of inerrancy and, indeed, argues that "[no] one conversant with twentieth century theology doubts that biblical inerrancy is one of the watershed issues of our time."[67] While such a claim may be true in regards to certain Evangelical theological circles, this is certainly not the case in Catholicism. There have, of course, been many works devoted to the proper understanding and role of Scripture over the past century. It is not at all clear, however, that the scholarly labels "trustworthy," "true," or "reliable" have the same connotation as "inerrancy" employed from within the context of US religious history. As Hahn demonstrated, Pius does use the phrase "except error," and then later in *Divino afflante spiritu* even the phrase "traditional teaching regarding the inerrancy of Sacred Scripture," yet, there is, again, some important historical situatedness that needs to be addressed, particularly regarding the rise of North American Christian Fundamentalism.[68]

Fundamentalism first emerges in the mid- and late nineteenth century in response to Darwinian evolutionary theory and the historical-critical method.[69] Darwin's *On the Origin of Species*, published in 1859, challenged not only the traditional Protestant interpretation of the Genesis creation story, but also called into question the very role of God in creation. In the wake of Darwin, the six days of Genesis became millions of years and the intentional creative acts of God were cast as simply the byproducts of blind processes. Most damningly, Darwin reduced the pinnacle of God's creation, humanity, to just another accidental movement of nature.

While evolution threatened the ontological significance of creation and humanity, historical criticism eroded the epistemological uniqueness of the biblical account. That is, the historical-critical approach was determined to evaluate the Scriptures in the same manner as any other historical text.[70] In doing so, the Scriptures were shown to have emerged out of a complex web of myth, differing traditions, and competing voices. Moreover, the Bible was shown to contain historical and scientific error, all of which undermined the Christian notion that the Scriptures provided humanity with an entirely perfect record of God's revelation.

66. Hahn, "Introduction," emphasis added.
67. Hahn, "For the Sake of Our Salvation: The Truth and Humility of God's Word," 33.
68. Pius XII, *Dinio afflante spiritu*, §46.
69. Trollinger and Trollinger, Jr., *Righting America at the Creation Museum*, 2.
70. Trollinger and Trollinger, Jr., *Righting America at the Creation Museum*, 2.

As the dual threats of evolution and historical criticism became more widely accepted in American scholarship and culture, Protestant Christians responded largely in one of two ways. Liberal Protestantism, on the one hand, worked to find ways to accommodate the contributions of evolution and criticism into their understanding of the Bible as the word of God in history through the embodied lives, concerns, biases, and even errors of the faithful of God.

The remainder of American Protestantism, however, responded to these new movements of science and literary criticism extremely negatively. Most significantly, these Christians responded with the doctrine of biblical inerrancy. First offered by Protestant theologians at Princeton University in the late nineteenth century, inerrancy holds that the Scriptures are the entirely perfect work of the Holy Spirit.[71] While such a commitment appeared to fly in the face of the now obvious errors of the biblical testimony, these scholars maintained that the absolute perfection of the Scriptures applied only to the original documents, that is, the autographs, and any apparent errors (of which there are in actuality very few) in the Bible we have today are the result of later copiers, translators, and interpreters. These autographs, however, are completely and utterly without error. Every historical, scientific, theological, even grammatical aspect of the Scriptures, in their original state, is as perfect as the person of Jesus Christ himself.

The inerrancy of Scripture is important to American Evangelical Christianity, however, not simply because it safeguards the testimony of the history of God's salvation of humanity, but also because it protects the integrity of the Bible's prophetic account of the future. Along with biblical inerrancy, a second doctrinal development of the nineteenth century is dispensational premillennialism. According to this Evangelical doctrine, the literal reading of Scripture, a corollary of inerrancy, provides the grounds for a division of history into seven different dispensations. In each dispensation or period, God tests humanity, humanity fails, and God's righteous judgment demands their punishment.[72] The current age will end with the Church betraying its calling, civilization reaching critical levels of immorality, the return of the Jews to Palestine, and Christ meeting the few remaining faithful in the sky to bring them to heaven.

All of this—the fight against Darwin, the rejection of historical-criticism, the commitment to biblical eschatological prophecy, even biblical inerrancy—is in service, however, of an even more foundational truth. Not only are the Scriptures perfect, they are also eminently accessible and

---

71. Trollinger and Trollinger, Jr., *Righting America at the Creation Museum*, 3.
72. Trollinger and Trollinger, Jr., *Righting America at the Creation Museum*, 3.

straightforward to each and every faithful Christian, without qualification. Martin Luther was correct that we do not need priests to approach the grace of God. What Luther failed to understand is that we also do not need theologians to tell us what the Bible says. The perfection of the Scriptures cannot ensure the inerrancy of God's revelation if we must depend upon the oftentimes errant intellectual contributions of the academy to receive it. Thus, the Scriptures must be equally accessible to all and any departure from the plain sense of the Scriptures is mere sinful hubris.

The development and subsequent embrace of Darwinian theory by many so-called "Christians" as well as the attacks of historical criticism on the truthfulness of Scripture encouraged Protestant Evangelical leaders to provide the remaining faithful with the marks of an authentic Christianity. Thus, in response to the spread of liberalism in Protestant Christianity, three-million copies of a twelve-volume series on the "fundamentals of the faith" were mailed out to Protestant ministers, seminary students, and editors of every denomination detailing conservative theological orthodoxy.[73] The core tenets of *The Fundamentals* and the fundamentalist movement that followed was the literal reading of Scripture and biblical inerrancy.

It is striking, however, that given fundamentalism's being born of the perceived threat of modernism, fundamentalism and historical criticism must be regarded as modern cousins. While wildly different in their methodologies and commitments, both arise out of the contributions of modernism. Moreover, both approaches are aimed at the same modernist goal, certainty. This point is made most clearly by Jason Hentschel in his *Evangelicals, Inerrancy, and the Quest for Certainty: Making Sense of our Battles for the Bible*:

> [Fundamentalists] may accuse liberal historical critics of subjectivism and the abuse of the biblical authors' intended meaning in those critics' attempt to get "behind" the text, but [fundamentalism's methodology] appears little different. . . . Both are drinking from the same modernist well in an attempt to quench the same modernist desire for certainty.[74]

This fundamentalist approach, which Hentschel cites as the grammatical-historical method, is one that maintains the integrity of biblical inerrancy and, consequently, inspiration, yet recognizes the exegetical need to

---

73. Trollinger and Trollinger, Jr., *Righting America at the Creation Museum*, 4.

74. Hentschel, *Evangelicals and the Quest for Certainty*, 127, fn. 104. Quotation changed to address fundamentalists in particular rather than simply Evangelicals (with permission from the author).

step beyond the particularities of the authors to the complete and uncompromised truth of the message of God contained within.

It is in this same modernist context that Hahn and his fellow contributors to this issue of *Letter & Spirit* (for the most part) strive toward certainty. To this end, they also appear to fail to recognize any difference between inspiration and truth. Brant Pitre, in his "The Mystery of God's Word: Inspiration, Inerrancy, and the Interpretation of Scripture," cites Vatican II's *Dei Verbum*. There, the document makes reference to the 1915 decree of the Pontifical Biblical Commission, which discusses the "Catholic dogma of the inerrancy (*inerrantia*) of Scripture."[75] In a later article in the volume, Germain Gresz claims that Vatican II, and specifically *Dei verbum*, defend the notion of inerrancy. In this work, Gresz uses the terms "inspiration" and "inerrancy" interchangeably and then goes on to argue that despite the Church's teaching, "many today who work at and study theology seem to assume that the writers might well have made mistakes or even told lies."[76] Whether such a statement is accurate is beyond the scope of the present discussion, but it betrays the duality with which he views the exegetical landscape. For Gresz, scholars either commit to the doctrine of inerrancy, or they believe that writers "made mistakes or even told lies." The Catholic tradition, however, rejects such oversimplification and offers the notion that the Scriptures contain exactly that which God intended to reveal. In that sense, the Catholic can commit to the trustworthiness of the Scriptures without intending to offer anything akin to what American Christian fundamentalism does.

Pablo Gadenz, in his "Magisterial Teaching on the Inspiration and Truth of Scriptures," argues in a similar vein. Here, he explores the logic of the doctrine of inspiration as put forth in both *Dei verbum* and *Providentissimus Deus* in order to demonstrate that the Church has always held that any charge of error of any sort in the Scriptures necessarily entails an attack on the perfection of God's own self. To this end, Gadenz holds up *Dei verbum*'s assertion that inspiration demands we "acknowledge the books of Scripture as teaching firmly, faithfully, and without error the truth that God wished to be recorded."[77] He sets this claim next to *Providentissimus Deus*'s assertion that "inspiration not only is essentially incompatible with error, but excludes and rejects it absolutely and necessarily" as it is impossible that God can speak that which is not true.[78] Gadenz concludes that the only pos-

---

75. Pitre, "The Mystery of God's Word," 51.
76. Greisz, "The Inspiration and Inerrancy of Scripture," 184.
77. Paul VI, *Dei verbum*, §11.
78. Leo XIII, *Providentissimus Deus*, 20.

sible deduction we can draw here is that the "truth or inerrancy of Scripture follows necessarily from its inspiration."[79]

In a later essay, Jeffrey Morrow comes to a similar conclusion, in his case, however, by assuming that inerrancy is the only remaining avenue to the recognition that historical criticism "by definition cannot demonstrate the mysteries of faith."[80] Peter Paul Zerafa, on the other hand, begins his discussion in his, "The Limits of Biblical Inerrancy," with the claim that "the dogma of inerrancy was not defined in special historical circumstances and in opposition to heretical views" but rather it was "the professed doctrine of the Church from the very beginning."[81] Morrow and Zerafa demonstrate the central difficulty of the discussion regarding a Catholic notion of inerrancy taking place in this important volume of *Letter & Spirit*. While every article maintains the centrality and importance of inerrancy, the relationship of inerrancy to more traditional language of trustworthiness, faithfulness, and truth remains unclear.

What unites this discussion, however, lies in Matthew Levering's "The Inspiration of Scripture." After providing an incredibly robust account of the history of biblical interpretation in the academy as well as the encyclical tradition since the rise of historical criticism in the nineteenth century, Levering notes that interest in the doctrine of biblical inspiration and its role in biblical interpretation has waned considerably since *Dei verbum* and Vatican II.[82] There are, he tells us, two notable exceptions to this. The first is Denis Farkasfalvy, the abbot of a Cistercian monastery, who argues that "inspiration and inerrancy" is best understood as offering a path of salvation to all of humanity rather than complete propositional accuracy.[83] While Levering finds his line of explanation compelling, Farkasfalvy's account, he argues, is incomplete without the contributions of the second exception to this tendency of disinterest in inspiration, Scott Hahn.[84]

For Levering, what Hahn provides is a much needed return to the contributions of *Divino afflante spiritu*, *Providentissimus deus*, and, most importantly, *Dei verbum*. Relying upon the contributions of these earlier documents, *Dei verbum* reminds us that divine inspiration, as an act of God, precludes error. This is attested to, Hahn contends, by the Church's

---

79. Gadenz, "Magisterial Teaching on the Inspiration and Truth of Scripture," 77–78.
80. Morrow, "The Modernist Crisis and the Shifting of Catholic Views on Biblical Inspiration," 280.
81. Zerafa, "The Limits of Biblical Inerrancy," 359.
82. Levering, "The Inspiration of Scripture," 311.
83. Levering, "The Inspiration of Scripture," 310.
84. Levering, "The Inspiration of Scripture," 312.

employment of the Scriptures liturgically. For Hahn, and for Levering, it makes no sense at all for the Church to rely upon the Scriptures in such a profound manner if the Scriptures are in error. The trustworthiness of the Scriptures, attested to by the encyclical tradition, upon which Catholic liturgy rests, Levering agrees, entails the inerrancy of the Scriptures.[85]

As discussed above, however, the logic of Levering and Hahn's argument is disrupted by the centrality of inerrancy in US fundamentalist history. Given this context, the contemporary understanding of inerrancy just does not follow from the Church's account of the trustworthiness of the Scriptures. And, thus, inerrancy in the mouths of Hahn and his colleagues just has a dramatically different connotation than *sine errore* or *inerrantia* and the like in the mouths of popes from almost a century ago and beyond. Looking to more recent explications of the relationship between inspiration and truth, the Pontifical Biblical Commission published "The Inspiration and Truth of Sacred Scripture" in 2014 wherein they note:

> As regards the truth of the Bible, we must above all be aware that although it covers many different subjects, the Bible really has a primary and central theme: God himself and salvation. There are many other documentary sources and many other disciplines providing reliable information on questions of every kind; the Bible, insofar as it is the Word of God, is the authoritative source of knowledge about God.[86]

As would be expected, the document speaks extremely highly of the integrity of Scripture, yet when given an opportunity to employ language of inerrancy, it instead offers the above description of biblical truth and opts for a discussion of trust and trustworthiness. The nature of inspiration varies, the document goes on to attest, due to the various manners by which God relates to the different writers. Thus, inspiration includes a rich phenomenology of the relationship between God and the human authors of Scripture.[87] Such a depiction, while profound, could hardly be cast as a simple reflection of Hahn and his compatriots' discussion of biblical inerrancy.

For all that, however, Hahn employs this terminology, and seeks to establish Ratzinger as its champion, in order to continue the narrative of a battle within Catholic scholarship between good and evil rather than simply an array of scholarly disagreement geared toward the greater understanding of truth. History matters and the fact that the history of inerrancy in the United States fundamentalist expression never appears in his discussion is

---

85. Levering, "The Inspiration of Scripture," 312.
86. Pontifical Biblical Commission, *The Inspiration and Truth of Sacred Scripture*, xx-xi.
87. Pontifical Biblical Commission, *The Inspiration and Truth of Sacred Scripture*, 53.

a serious oversight, particularly given his own conversion from American Evangelical Christianity. It is critical that, in our work as theologians, and, more importantly, in our own walks of faith, we see the role that history plays in our own story.

Which returns us to the third concern with Hahn's presentation of Ratzinger, and the most troubling. While the decision to not engage, as discussed above, the historical context of Ratzinger's rebuke of historical criticism and to employ his use of the Soloviev story as a warning against allies of the enemy within the ranks of contemporary theologians might simply be a matter of scholarly disagreement, explicit misrepresentation of his writings is not. While only alluded to in *Covenant and Communion*, a favorite quote of both Hahn and his colleagues in the St. Paul Center is one from an address given in Lyons, France in 1983 (and then published as an article entitled "Crisis in Catechesis" that same year) in which Ratzinger, again addressing the abuses of historical-criticism, proclaims, "In fact, dogma is by definition nothing other than an interpretation of Scripture. But it is an interpretation which has sprung from the faith over the centuries, unable, so it would appear, to be in accord with the understanding of the texts arrived at by the historical-critical method."[88]

It is readily apparent, at first glance, why such a quote would be returned to time and again by Hahn and his colleagues given our above discussion. Interestingly, however, every time this quote appears there is a subtle, but critical modification. Found in Hahn's *The Last Supper*, the quote is rendered with an ellipses in the place of "But it is an interpretation." In his introduction to the *Ignatius Study Bible*, on the St. Paul Center's discussion of the Catholic interpretation of Scripture, as well as in several postings of this passage on social media sites, the first half of the quote, "In fact, dogma is by definition nothing other than an interpretation of Scripture," is offered without any allusion to the second portion of Ratzinger's statement.

It is completely natural and proper for scholars at times to make determinations as to how much of a quotation to include. Yet, the language that Ratzinger employs in the second sentence of this quotation clearly provides qualifications to the first. A discussion with my wife in which I offer, "I am on my way home" but choose to omit "but I am going to stop by the store on my way," as any married person will agree, is the difference between Beth calmly awaiting my return and frantically calling wondering if my car is upside down on the side of the road somewhere. That is to say, the "but it is an interpretation" of Ratzinger's discussion matters! Rather than Ratzinger endorsing the notion that Catholic dogma is another term for

88. Ratzinger, "Crisis in Catechesis," 8.

biblical interpretation, this omitted portion renders all of Catholic tradition an exercise in "biblical theology," and this omission simply an intentional misrepresentation in the service of inerrancy. It is the difference, in short, between Ratzinger understanding himself as correcting a tradition that has lost sight of its connection to the Scriptures on the one hand and reinforcing the notion that all of Catholic tradition is always already pursuing the revelation of God in the Scriptures on the other.

John Henry Newman, in his *An Essay on the Development of Christian Doctrine*, provides an account of how we might determine whether a development of Christian doctrine is authentic. To that end, he offers us seven notes of genuine development of an idea. These are: preservation of type, continuity of principles, power of assimilation, logical sequence, anticipation of its future, conservative action upon its past, and chronic vigor. It was Newman's hope that by employing these notes he would be able to locate the faith of the apostles in the very different world he inhabited.

For preservation of type, Newman is looking for those ideas that, while perhaps changed in their external presentation, continue to maintain an internal sameness.[89] That is, while ideas can develop and their implementation change over time, they must demonstrate a continual presence of a central concept. Continuity of principles, Newman's second note, seeks to determine whether the idea has developed according to the same guiding principles with which it was first introduced.[90] The third note of authentic development, power of assimilation, looks for the strength by which an idea takes hold in the minds of the faithful.[91] His fourth note, and one that is critical for the discussion taking place here, is logical sequence. That is, a genuine development must be recognized as the necessary outcome of the growth of an idea along certain principles such that it could not have become anything different than what it did. This logical sequence, Newman writes, "is a security for the faithfulness of intellectual developments" and is what allows us to find with confidence the contributions of the apostles alive in the minds of the faithful today.[92] A doctrine, then, is likely to be a true development and not a corruption to the extent that it can be recognized as the logical offspring of its original teaching.[93]

---

89. Newman, *An Essay on the Development of Christian Doctrine*, 178.
90. Newman, *An Essay on the Development of Christian Doctrine*, 181.
91. Newman, *An Essay on the Development of Christian Doctrine*, 188.
92. Newman, *An Essay on the Development of Christian Doctrine*, 189–90.
93. Newman, *An Essay on the Development of Christian Doctrine*, 195.

In a similar vein, the fifth note is the ability then to anticipate the doctrine's future. Such a notion recognizes that doctrines do not remain static; that, in fact, the resistance of a doctrine to grow and flourish is itself a sign of corruption. Yet, the sixth note, conservative action upon its past, tempers the notion inherent in the fifth. While it is important for ideas to develop, it is crucial that those changes are a gradual and slow development that moves with great care in order to safeguard the notions and principles that guided their past.[94] And lastly, the seventh note of authentic development for Newman is what he refers to as an idea's chronic vigor. The chronic vigor of a doctrine is, to put it plainly, the unwillingness of that doctrine to be defeated. While there may at times be setbacks or even decay in how a doctrine is employed, the final note of genuine development is that the idea just continues to drive forward and bring other ideas and developments along in its wake.

For Newman, the search for that most critical authentic development, the Idea of Christianity, eventually brought him to the doors of the Catholic faith. Yet, while he found a faith that accorded with that for which he was looking, it was the history of the faith that assured him that he found the right place. What distinguishes Catholicism from other expressions of Christian faith, Newman argued, was that the history of the faith belonged firmly and wholly to Catholicism:

> History is not a creed or a catechism, it gives lessons rather than rules; still no one can mistake its general teaching in this matter, whether he accept it or stumble at it. Bold outlines and broad masses of colour rise out of the records of the past. They may be dim, they may be incomplete; but they are definite. And this one thing at least is certain; whatever history teaches, whatever it omits, whatever it exaggerates or extenuates, whatever it says and unsays, at least the Christianity of history is not Protestantism.[95]

Whether Newman is accurate in this regard is, naturally, beyond the scope of our discussion here. Yet, what cannot be denied is that Catholicism is irrevocably committed to the faith being carried and strengthened throughout history. "To be deep in history," Newman argued, "is to cease to be a Protestant."[96] What remains is to answer where this leaves theological writing inattentive to history.

---

94. Newman, *An Essay on the Development of Christian Doctrine*, 200.
95. Newman, *An Essay on the Development of Christian Doctrine*, 7.
96. Newman, *An Essay on the Development of Christian Doctrine*, 8.

4

The Fundamentals of a Truly Catholic America

THE PONTIFICATE OF THE now St. John Paul II is among the most celebrated of any in the history of the Catholic Church. Coming off the heels of the massive developments of the Second Vatican Council, John Paul II is remembered as the pope who transformed the traditional role and demeanor of the office; thrusting what was often regarded by the non-Catholic world as an unimportant and archaic position into international celebrity and prominence.[1] He met with U.S. Presidents Jimmy Carter, Ronald Reagan, George H. W. Bush, Bill Clinton, and George W. Bush in the Vatican. He was famously sought out by Bob Dylan and U2's Bono and sat down with Rosa Parks, Nelson Mandela, the Dali Lama, and Queen Elizabeth II. He wrote thirteen encyclicals and a myriad of apostolic letters and exhortation, including: *Centesimus anuus*, an updating of the Church's Catholic Social Teaching a century after the promulgation of *Rerum novarum*; *Fides et ratio*, a discourse on the relationship between faith and reason particularly in light of the contributions of science and historical methods; and, *Veritatis splendor*, a recommitment and explanation of the fundamentals of Catholic ideology. More than any other pope of recent history, John Paul II brought the theological, moral, and ideological commitments of the Catholic tradition into the modern world.

1. Sr. Mary Ann Walsh, "The Life and Ministry of Saint. John Paul II."

An interesting, yet little discussed, contribution is his *Ecclesia in America*, an apostolic exhortation given at Mexico City on January 22nd, 1999 that addressed the strengths and failings of the Catholic Church in the Americas. His exhortation begins by highlighting the clear desire of the Church in America to lead men and women to encounter with Christ.[2] The place of encounter with authentic conversion and communion, rather than merely in abstraction, is, first, "the Sacred Scriptures read in the light of the Tradition, the Fathers and the Magisterium, and more deeply understood through meditation and prayer."[3] The second place of encounter he offers is in the sacred liturgy. Most compellingly, then, the "leading men and women of the continent to encounter Christ" has its genesis not in the *Other* but rather in us as the body of Christ. This is due to the fact that the third location of encounter, and that to which the first two guide us, is in "persons, especially the poor with whom Christ identifies himself."[4]

In our encountering Christ in the person, particularly the poor, John Paul II draws our attention to the position of the poor. In the Americas, we must recognize both the reality of fascist governments that have furthered the suffering of the poor as well as the spread of democratic political systems that aid in the alleviation of that suffering.[5] Yet, even in those cases in which dictatorial regimes have been replaced with governments respectful of the rights and dignity of persons, we must always be cognizant of the ways in which the sins of the past continue to yield consequences for the future. For the pope, this is most clearly present in the economic oppression faced by the poor and working class as well as the indebtedness of these countries freed from authoritarianism by those who aided them in the name of profit and globalization.[6]

Conversion, in this context, must be understood as a rejection of the separation between our faith and works in our daily response to the universal call to holiness.[7] That is, we are renewed not just through the activities of our practices of faith but also in attuning ourselves to see the faith made real in the fight for the poor and marginalized in every sphere of life. Understanding ourselves as truly the sons and daughters of God "means attending to all the needs of our neighbor."[8] This implies that "parishes are called to be

---

2. John Paul II, *Ecclesia in America*, 21.
3. John Paul II, *Ecclesia in America*, 22.
4. John Paul II, *Ecclesia in America*, 23–24.
5. John Paul II, *Ecclesia in America*, 34.
6. John Paul II, *Ecclesia in America*, 36, 39.
7. John Paul II, *Ecclesia in America*, 44.
8. John Paul II, *Ecclesia in America*, 45.

welcoming and fraternal" in their service to the community and "attentive to the cultural diversity" of the people they serve.[9]

To this end, in a land marked by corruption, unbridled consumerism, and greed, laypersons are called "to embody deeply evangelical values as mercy, forgiveness, honesty, transparency of heart and patience in difficult situations."[10] This is most clearly needed, John Paul II tells us, in the plight of women, minorities, and immigrants. We must recognize the deeply troubling "feminine side of poverty,"[11] in which women are the most likely to bear the brunt of economic and social oppression, particularly among minority and immigrant communities. Here, we must be "a vigilant advocate, defending against any unjust restriction the natural right of individual persons to move freely within their own nation and from one nation to another."[12] The face of American conversion and renewal is the commitment to work for the good of all, particularly the poor, marginalized, ostracized, and forgotten. And in this work, people of all faiths, but particularly Muslims, Jews, and Christians in light of their shared history, must see themselves drawn together in the fight for the common good.[13] That is, "the goal of the Church is to ensure that *no one* is marginalized," and we align ourselves with those in the human community with whom we share this sacred duty.[14]

Critical to this conversion and renewal is the sacrament of reconciliation, a central concern throughout his pontificate. The Catholic Church, which embraces people of every nation, race, and language, is called to be the "living sign of the unity of the human family" in this world that is so often "marked by ideological, ethnic, economic and cultural divisions."[15] In the call to unity of the human family, which has as its foundation the conjugal relationship between husband and wife, we must battle against the insidious forces endangering the family unit, which includes "divorce, the spread of abortion, infanticide, and the contraceptive mentality."[16] The sacrament of reconciliation, however, reminds us that in this fight for unity and solidarity, the work begins in ourselves and not the *other*.

---

9. John Paul II, *Ecclesia in America*, 69.
10. John Paul II, *Ecclesia in America*, 76.
11. John Paul II, *Ecclesia in America*, 79.
12. John Paul II, *Ecclesia in America*, 109.
13. John Paul II, *Ecclesia in America*, 88.
14. John Paul II, *Ecclesia in America*, 97, emphasis added.
15. John Paul II, *Ecclesia in America*, 54.
16. John Paul II, *Ecclesia in America*, 81.

The culmination of Scott Hahn's body of work rests in his answer to the problem of modern society. In his *The First Society: The Sacrament of Matrimony and the Restoration of the Social Order*, just as John Paul II did in *Ecclessia in America*, Hahn sets out to provide the Catholic response to the immorality and degradation of modern Western culture. It is this "culture in crisis from top to bottom" that has forced Hahn to address the "social erosion effected by secularism and liberalism."[17] In contrast with John Paul II's emphasis on the sacrament of reconciliation, Hahn offers that the only solution to the ills of modern society is a return to the sacrament of marriage. Before we delve into Hahn's solution to the ills of society, however, it is critical that we understand exactly how immoral that society has become.

The distinguishing marks of a society in free-fall are, for Hahn, the lack of stable families and the breach of family ties.[18] In looking, then, for those most pernicious aspects of secular liberalism, Hahn centers on four: abortion, birth control, no-fault divorce, and non-traditional marriage. While discussing each of these in different contexts and in different places, he is sure to make evident that these four are simultaneously *symptoms* and *causes* of Western societal decline. We will examine each of the four in turn, demonstrating how each function both as symptom and cause.

As we would expect with any Catholic discussion of modern society, for Hahn, the legalization of abortion stands as one of the most horrific innovations of recent history. "It is the intentional killing of an innocent human person," he tells us, "But it is a very particular type of killing—one that rends the social fabric in uniquely destructive ways."[19] The position of a parent intentionally choosing to end the life of their child tears apart the most basic relationship of society in a violent and foundational manner. For Hahn, this breach of the natural familial bond, which obligates us to love, protect, and nurture our children, necessarily then also undermines every other relational structure of a properly functioning society. If we cannot see our way to honoring the first society we ever experienced, the parent-child relationship, then Hahn believes it will be impossible for us to go on to fully appreciate our level of obligation to the poor, the sick, the elderly, or the immigrant.

Moreover, while abortion breaches that most basic of societal bonds, the fact that it does so for the sake of convenience, the realization of subjectively perceived identity and/or the pursuit of wealth, makes it even more destructive. That is, abortion rips apart that most important parent-to-child relationship for the sake of reimagining sex as disconnected from its natural

---

17. Hahn, *The First Society*, xvii.
18. Hahn, *The First Society*, 38.
19. Hahn, *The First Society*, 151.

end of procreation, the unwillingness to understand oneself as parent, and the massive profitability of institutions like Planned Parenthood that have turned abortion into a billion-dollar industry. And in so doing, abortion both reflects and encourages a relativistic worldview in which any moral or societal duty can be cast aside in exchange for the facade of *choice*.

The horrors of abortion are echoed, for Hahn, in the normalization and proliferation of contraception. The assumption that sex is and ought to be sterile "provides the foundations for many other errors in thinking about sex, both personally and politically."[20] The natural end of human sexuality residing in procreation, as enshrined in Church teaching, is a constant reminder that we were created for something outside of ourselves. The very Catholic notion that sex was made, first and foremost, for the participation with God in the creation of new people is a constant reminder, especially in our most intimate moment, that we must always be looking outside of ourselves, toward the good and flourishing of those with whom we share the various levels of society.[21]

The view of the world that contraception promotes is one in which the individual must be assumed to be primary, sterile, and self-seeking. Any derivation from this societal expectation must be regarded as, at best, supererogatory, but more likely, simply another free act of the will that bears with it no moral weight. Birth control dismembers the communal act of creation with God as well as furthers the inward focus of the individual, which leads to the isolation and alienation that is so clearly plaguing modern, liberal society. In virtue of its being ordered toward procreation, sex ought to be recognized as the one thing we do with our bodies that is most uniquely connected with the common good.[22] In today's individualistic culture, however, contraception marks a rejection of a pursuit of the common good.

If birth-control is dissolving the bonds of society at its most generative level, it is the emergence of no-fault divorce that is tearing down society at its most unitive. We have no chance of instilling in our children the ability to "live out the reciprocal duties of solidarity" if the very place where they first

---

20. Hahn, *The First Society*, 89.

21. Hahn, *The First Society*, 89. It should be noted that Hahn goes on to claim that the belief that the primary end of the sex act is procreative and not both procreative and unitive is "vigorously reaffirmed both in *Casti connubii* and, several decades later, in Pope Paul VI's famous *Humanae vitae*." While both *Casti connubii* and *Humanae vitae* agree that the "primary end of marriage is the procreation and the education of children" (*CC*) and that "marriage and conjugal love are by their nature ordained toward the procreation and education of children" (*HV*), neither indicate that the unitive aspect of the marital act is secondary to procreation.

22. Hahn, *The First Society*, 93.

learn self-sacrifice and commitment offers neither.[23] No-fault divorce has taught society that there are no ties that truly bind us together as a community. In the decades since no-fault divorce was introduced, Hahn reminds us, divorce rates have sky-rocketed to more than 50 percent.[24]

Secular culture's embrace of no-fault divorce reduces the marital bond to one of mere convenience. This rejection of marriage as a sacred covenant has resulted in a generation that is largely unable to recognize selflessness and commitment. Even more critical, Hahn concludes, "once we've lost the meaning and purpose of marriage, anything can go."[25] In the years since marriage was gutted in the 1970s, we have seen the emergence of plural marriages, wed leases—temporary but renewable marriage contracts—and recently even self-marriages. The most troubling consequence of the downfall of the idea of marriage, however, is same-sex marriage.

"Any society in which the idea of same-sex 'marriage' can gain a foothold," Hahn mourns, "has already lost its marriage culture."[26] It is in this last and most pernicious mark of an immoral society that we can begin to understand just how far humanity has fallen. In the embrace of a complete individualism that offers the fiction that we are able to radically self-identify, the family as the foundation of society has been shifted to the whims and failings of individual people. The idea that we are all able to decide for ourselves our sexual attractions, gender, and even race demonstrates the belief that there are no real ties that bind us together.[27] In the name of sexual and marital freedom, we have allowed our society to become saturated in broken families, pornography, all manner of disordered actions and desires, and, most tragically, "intense feeling[s] of alienation and loneliness that pervades especially younger and poorer communities."[28]

Once again, in these four marks of a society in free-fall—abortion, contraception, no-fault divorce, and non-traditional marriage—Hahn sees both causes of our increasingly immoral society as well as symptoms of a culture that has already fallen. That is, for Hahn, these four horsemen of western society's apocalypse did not entirely create the broken society in which we now live. Rather, these ills were let loose on us by our walking away from the sacrament of marriage. Marriage, as God created it, was and

---

23. Hahn, *The First Society*, 152.
24. Hahn, *The First Society*, 123.
25. Hahn, *The First Society*, 124.
26. Hahn, *The First Society*, 124.
27. Hahn, *The First Society*, 32.
28. Hahn, *The First Society*, 97.

is the first society in which humans ever participated.[29] It is the first place that we find ourselves brought together to work for a common good outside ourselves. It is the first place that we realize our *imago dei* in the coming together in the creation of children. It is the first place that we recognize our capacity for kenotic or self-denying love and care for another. In our learning to love a partner, a child, and good for us beyond just me, we begin to claim the trinitarian end for which we were created. Same-sex "marriage," as Hahn writes it, did not create our immoral society; instead, it was our willingness to trade the covenantal understanding of marriage for one of contract, convenience, and freedom that brought about the conditions for the poisonous culture we now inhabit. Moreover, it is only in the return to the sacrament of marriage that society can be restored.

Hahn begins his discussion of sacramental marriage with a somewhat surprising claim: marriage is impossible. This impossibility of marriage appears to fly in the face, he recognizes, of the strong, committed marriages that many of us experience for ourselves and see reflected in many of the families around us. This, however, is to misunderstand the sacrament of marriage. In simply using the language of sacramental marriage, we are forced to recognize that there is non-sacramental marriage, which we might be more comfortable with referring to as simply natural marriage. What we are called to in the very idea of marriage has been placed out of reach by the introduction of sin in creation. It is only through the grace of God, given to us in the sacrament of marriage, that we can truly take up the mantle of "two made one."

As society depicts it, marriage is, first and foremost, civil. That is, the reality of marriage is in its being made "official" in the form of a marriage license, and any religious aspect of marriage is an added layer that we wrap around this civil understanding.[30] This, Hahn argues, is not the case. Before marriage was ever understood legally, it was natural. The fact of our creation as male and female and instinct towards community makes it evident that marriage is natural and not an invention of the state. Just as humanity has a nature, bestowed upon us by God in the creation of the world, so does marriage.[31] This is not to say that what was intended for marriage is mirrored in the natural world as the instinct to procreation in nature is often also "red in tooth and claw." What makes marriage natural is that God gifted us with marriage in the beginning of all things and, thus, God's intention in the institution of marriage remains with us. Marriage, sacramental or not,

---

29. Hahn, *The First Society*, 23.
30. Hahn, *The First Society*, 39.
31. Hahn, *The First Society*, 40.

is and always has been marked with three essential attributes: "permanence, exclusivity, and openness of life."[32]

What makes marriage impossible, then, is our inability always to embody these characteristics. Through marriage we are to help our partners achieve their created end. The permanence, exclusivity, and openness to life that marks marriage are the conditions necessary for spouses to aid their partners toward that end. And, it turns out, we cannot do this on our own. If we look at the Law in the Old Testament, we find that even Moses recognized the incredible difficulty of natural marriage and he "was compelled to make exceptions."[33] It is not until the sacrament of marriage is made available to us that marriage truly became possible, both personally and as the foundation of society. "The sacrament brings to bear the grace of God," Hahn argues, "that is necessary to live out even the basic requirements of natural marriage."[34] It is not, then, our failing at natural marriage that has brought about this societal apocalypse, but rather the fact that we were gifted the sacrament of marriage, built society upon the foundation of sacramental marriage, and then turned away from the sacrament and rejected its nature.

Thus, while abortion, contraception, no-fault divorce, and non-traditional marriage have certainly played a role in the continued fall of moral norms and societal structures, the cause of our current predicament, according to Hahn, is our rejection of the nature of marriage. He demonstrates this by pointing to those aspects of the collapse of our society that predate these four moral shifts. All human societies eventually mirror the form and structure of the families that compose them.[35] A few generations ago, neighborhoods and communities were built for families living interconnected lives rather than atomized individuals. Sidewalks, streets, and public spaces were suitable for visits with friends or for the many children to come together to play.

Walking through contemporary community developments, on the other hand, we find a lot of similar features, yet with very different ends. Rather than open spaces for children to play games of cops and robbers, we find paved patios for sipping coffee. Communities built around Catholic Churches from a century or more ago are now centered around business

---

32. Hahn, *The First Society*, 41. This teaching regarding the nature of marriage is confirmed in Pius XI's *Casti Connubii* and as well as Paul VI's *Humane Vitae*. In both documents, the notion that marriage shared these three attributes in the institution of marriage in the story of Adam and Eve and continues to be understood in that manner is recognized as a central feature of Catholic tradition.

33. Hahn, *The First Society*, 43.
34. Hahn, *The First Society*, 44.
35. Hahn, *The First Society*, 28.

and entertainment, while those same Churches sit empty and forgotten, haunting specters of everything we have abandoned.[36]

When the connective tissue of society, marriage, disintegrates, society is left with only the state and the market. As we turned our focus inward on individuals and nuclear, independent families, our society lost its interest in marriage and family. We privileged work and money over common goods. As we determined that marriage and family were not foundational, we began to require longer work hours for relatively smaller wages, both spouses to work outside the home, and profitability to reward the rich rather than support the family. Hegemonic consumer capitalism demands the market to be solely regarded as the source of identity formation.[37] Rather than being marked by the family and community within which we were formed, we clothe ourselves in brand loyalty and market forces. Our isolation has rendered us anxious, desperate, and insecure. Moreover, as has always been the nature of sin, the despair wrought by our turning away from a culture of marriage itself casts us ever deeper into anxiety and loneliness.

Society has been gutted of its very substance—stable marriage and family ties. The solution, of course, is a

> reemergence of a robust culture of marriage, where husbands and wives are supported in their vocation to a permanent covenant of faithfulness and, God willing, childbearing. Nothing short of this will do. But this will require more than having nice marriages portrayed on sitcoms and government programs to counsel young couples. It will also require a public understanding of the *sacramentality* of marriage—that marriage is more than just a notarized contract, but a covenant in which the Lord of Heaven and Earth participates.[38]

While such a solution, Hahn concludes, is obvious, it does not in itself tell us how to go about achieving it. Where do we go? To the same place that we have always gone for refuge and strength, Jesus. If we look to the Holy Family, we see that Mary in her perfection and Joseph in his fallenness both perpetually turn their unified gaze toward their holy son.[39] The one time that their focus slipped, Christ disappeared only to be found "in [his] Father's house."[40] Even Mary, the perfect Mother of God, did not always fully understand what she needed to be for her son. Mary's perfection was

---

36. Hahn, *The First Society*, 29.
37. Hahn, *The First Society*, 34.
38. Hahn, *The First Society*, 38.
39. Hahn, *The First Society*, 52.
40. Luke 2:48–49.

not demonstrated in her always understanding, but in her allowing herself to be taught, and by the end of her life we find her where we ought to be, at the foot of the cross. If we allow ourselves to wrestle with this incredible example of the Holy Family, we learn that through family, his family, was the only way that Christ could be brought to where he could win our salvation.[41]

In recognizing that family was the avenue through which God could enact God's will, we are forced to confess the necessity of traditional family and sacramental marriage. The Holy Family's poverty, relative insignificance, and simplicity did not disqualify them from Christ's choosing in a manner that their brokenness, individualness, and unfaithfulness would have. Mary and Joseph were bound together by the shared responsibility of their holy child and their constant communion with their Son who was God strengthened them to live out their duty with love and charity.[42] Insofar as we seek to restore society, it is critical, Hahn exhorts, that we insist upon the same for the families that make up our society.

This sacramental society, then, can only be achieved by insisting, not just in our own marriages being sacramental, but all marriages. There can be no quarter, no peace, with that which poisons society and draws us further and further from God. When we look at civilization throughout history, we see that many of the same pieces were in place. There have always been temptations, selfishness, sin, and evil. There have always been threats to society and family that brought about anxiety and isolation. Marriage and family, however, "have never been unrecognizable—until, perhaps, this moment, when even the most enduring conventions, such as the necessity of opposite-sex couples, are being dismissed."[43] The root difference between our society today and those of the past, Hahn concludes, is the foundation of sacramental marriage.

As we discussed above, to return to sacramental marriage is to return to the example of the Holy Family. According to Catholic tradition, however, the Holy Family is not simply an example for us. In the sacramental, communal life of the Church we are invited into Christ's family as brothers and sisters. Thus, if we seek to truly understand what a society rooted in the sacrament of marriage would look like, we need not look any further than the Church. The marks then of a sacramental society are the same as those professed by the Church in the Nicene Creed.

First, the Church is *one*. Hahn explains that in our society, which is predicated on the illusions of choice and freedom, the presence of as many

---

41. Hahn, *The First Society*, 54.
42. Hahn, *The First Society*, 56.
43. Hahn, *The First Society*, 66.

singular, individual "goods" as possible is championed as a sign of progress. Such a kaleidoscope of goods, however, only furthers feelings of uncertainty and insecurity. Conversely, the Church's oneness, that is its unfractured existence and singular offer of true goodness in the sacrifice of Christ, is a reprieve from the never-ending pressure to consume and own more. Moreover, the unity of the Church is also an answer to our society that is now so deeply divided along political, social, economic, and ethnic lines. "There is not," Hahn argues, "a Republican church or a Democratic church, a rich church or a poor church, a white church or a black church."[44] The Church is one because our God is one.

Second, the Church is *holy*. While the secular world ranges between empty self-pity and perverse self-congratulations concerning the apparent meaningless of existence, it is the Church that alone bridges the divide between human and divine. The uniqueness of the Church, Hahn extols, lies in its being constituted by humanity while being oriented toward the eternal.[45] It is only through the Church that we find a purpose that goes beyond self-interest.

Third, the Church is *catholic*. The Church is predicated on a radical inclusiveness that our society has only ever pretended to offer. Unwavering in its solidarity, it is the Church that models true community for our world divided by political ideology, economic disparity, and ethnocentric prejudice. In fact, it is "the claim inherent in the Church's catholicity—that there is a common good to *every* member of society, and that good rests in the Church," Hahn explains, that "may be the most jarring to modern ears, but also the most important and appealing."[46] It is only in the Church that every single member of the human community is loved, accepted, and cherished.

And finally, the Church is *apostolic*. Hahn notes the irony that our secular society is currently obsessed with notions of sustainability, yet they ignore the only truly sustainable aspect of our world, the Church handed by Christ to the apostles and carried unified and unbroken through two millennia of human history.[47] More importantly than the Church's endurance since the time of Christ is the promise that it perdures until Christ returns. The permanence and steadfastness of the Church renders it the only appropriate foundation for social order. The "answer to the modern despair over whether anything can be truly lasting" is the Church.[48]

---

44. Hahn, *The First Society*, 75.
45. Hahn, *The First Society*, 76.
46. Hahn, *The First Society*, 76.
47. Hahn, *The First Society*, 77.
48. Hahn, *The First Society*, 77.

In that our marriages and families exemplify the Church, and, indeed, comprise the Church, then they must reflect its vision of oneness, holiness, catholicity, and apostolicity. Sacramental marriage, as a foundation for sacramental society, must be one in its exclusive commitment to the unity of husband and wife, holy in its being centered on the divine perfection of God's love, catholic in that we must hold that God's plan for marriage holds for every human person, and apostolic in that it is bolstered by the families from which the partners were formed and its end is in the generations born from it. It is in its representation of the Church that the family is a "universal hermeneutic—that is, an interpretive key that is accessible to everyone—for thinking about and understanding human societies."[49] According to Hahn, it is precisely this conception of society, however, that is under fire.

In the face of our deeply sick and self-destructive society, the imperative to live the sacrament of marriage and, more, to insist upon the sacrament of marriage, is not something on which we can compromise. Our culture is not wrong in recognizing that our moral commitments and actions have an inherently public commitment, Hahn contends, "it's just committed to enforcing a disordered morality."[50] The proper response, then, is not to allow that which is inherently public to be relegated to the private, but to insist on what is right and good. Whether it is in regards to businesses or individuals refusing to respect new concepts of gender and sexuality or a florist's conscience not permitting her to arrange flowers for a same-sex ceremony,[51] the move toward a society that lives a sacramental society necessitates our unfailing commitment to the common good that we all share (even those of other faiths or no faith) in God.[52]

For Hahn, the catholicity of the Church's social vision cannot be relegated to the good of individuals or nuclear families:

> First, of course, the Body of Christ beckons all human beings to the divine embrace without prejudice or preference. But universality also means that the Church is not just "religious": her teaching and authority touch all aspects of human experience-social, cultural, economic, political, and so on. It is precisely this catholicity that points to a way forward for a disintegrating civilization.[53]

---

49. Hahn, *The First Society*, 83.
50. Hahn, *The First Society*, 91.
51. Hahn, *The First Society*, 90–91.
52. Hahn, *The First Society*, 83.
53. Hahn, *The First Society*, 151.

In recognition of the implications of the Church's catholicity, Hahn concludes, we have a duty to "advance the liberty of the Catholic Church to fulfill its fully catholic mission in all areas of life."[54] And lest we be confused, Hahn goes to great effort to make sure that we understand this in the most concrete possible terms. In order to save our depraved society, Hahn argues that we are to carry the sacramental nature of marriage into every aspect of society. We must demand that "liturgy and politics cannot be disentangled," and recognize that what we celebrate in Mass is also that around which all of society should be ordered.[55] In that both serve to bring the sacramental grace of God to others, "marriage and priesthood are radically *political* vocations."[56]

The recognition that the priesthood is, in fact, a political vocation, entails that modernity's separation of Church and State is a lie. We must insist that the proper depiction of the division between religious and secular is not Church and State, but rather clergy and laity.[57] Hahn provides an insight into exactly how such a notion is to be borne out:

> If it is the nature of the civil authority to pursue the common good, and if it is in the nature of sex that it uniquely pertains to the common good [sc., which it does], then it is entirely within the purview of the state to regulate sex. More than that: any government that takes the common good seriously will take an interest in sexual behavior—and not just grave violations such as assault.... [However] a state *might* choose not to criminalize sexual sin not because there is some value in the sin or in the freedom to commit it (there is never a right to sin), but because enforcement of a criminal statute would lead to greater evils.[58]

Hahn recognizes the discomfort that such an imperative might bring us, but that discomfort changes neither the truth nor our duty. The Church is "the perfect society" and therefore our duty is to "advance the liberty of the Catholic Church to fulfill its fully catholic mission in all areas of life."[59] Underneath all of this, however, is a troubling certainty.

As we discussed briefly in the previous chapter, Christian fundamentalism emerged in the early twentieth century in response to the dual threats of Darwinian evolutionary theory and historical-critical methodology. In

---

54. Hahn, *The First Society*, 157.
55. Hahn, *The First Society*, 170.
56. Hahn, *The First Society*, 171.
57. Hahn, *The First Society*, 172.
58. Hahn, *The First Society*, 94–95. Interpolation and emphasis added.
59. Hahn, *The First Society*, 157.

the century since the circulation of *The Fundamentals*, much ink has been spilled concerning the marks of fundamentalism and its formation. Despite the varied perspectives on the phenomenon of Christian fundamentalism, most contributions have centered on one of three characteristics as fundamentalism's most defining feature: premillennialism, militancy, or literalism and inerrancy.[60]

A driving concern of virtually every form of Christian fundamentalism is the return of Christ and the looming apocalypse, which is always very nearly here. In the century preceding *The Fundamentals*, Evangelical Christians in Britain and the United States had become convinced that they were beginning to witness the events foretold in the prophetic books of Daniel and Revelation. The recent French Revolution of the eighteenth century, particularly the banishment of the pope, began to be interpreted as the "deadly wound" on one of the heads of the beast that emerges from the sea in Revelation 13,[61] a clear sign that human history had conclusively reached the end times. With this firm point of departure, these Christians became obsessed with determining just how the world would end and God's people saved. Given the literalistic exegesis with which they approached the Scriptures, great interest was placed on Revelation's thousand years of peace that was, in some way, to coincide with the return of Christ. While it had long been taught that the second coming would come at some far distant point in the future, with the developments of the French Revolution and the "wounding" of Catholicism, a school of thought emerged claiming that a faithful reading of biblical prophecy made it clear that Christ's return was imminent, most likely within their lifetime, and that it would in fact precede the millennium of peace that was to come.[62]

This premillennial perspective began to dominate Protestant Evangelicalism, particularly in the United States, and was central to the fundamentalist movement which emerged in the 1920s. Reinforced by World War I and the return of Palestine to the Jewish people, premillennialism assumed that the message born of a literal reading of the biblical books of prophecy indicated that humanity was completely incapable of bringing about any true and lasting social progress and, more tragically, that the Church would

---

60. The 2015 dissertation by Jason Hentschel, referred to previously, "Evangelicals and the Quest for Certainty," is an excellent book-length discussion of precisely this issue. While Hentschel and I differ slightly on the roll that Reid played versus Hume in the development of this fundamentalist epistemology, his discussion is an excellent resource for those who seek to delve into this issue more deeply.

61. Sandeen, *The Roots of Fundamentalism*, 7.

62. Sandeen, *The Roots of Fundamentalism*, 12.

be unable to stem the tide of evil that was in the process of rolling over the world, their particular society, and even the Church itself.[63]

As premillennialism was assumed in much of American fundamentalism, the fundamentalist Bible institutes and other fundamentalist institutions taught that what separates the saved from the unfaithful was the literal reading of Scripture. It is all well and good that the Christian is able to provide a shape and clarity to the coming apocalypse as well as the path of salvation from it, but it is the fact that the Bible is completely and utterly without error and our commitment to reading the Scriptures in their plainest and most common sense that allows us that eschatological insight in the first place. In her *The Bible Tells Them So*, Kathleen Boone provides a compelling analysis of fundamentalist exegesis that resides at the core of its ideology. Boone recognizes that "virtually all persons who identify themselves as fundamentalists are premillennialists,"[64] yet she argues that the center of fundamentalist discourse is a Bible that can be interpreted literally, given its inerrancy, that provides fundamentalism its power.[65] A commitment to the belief that a faithful, literal reading of the completely perfect Word of God, allows the individual Christian a mastery over life's most existentially terrifying difficulties. Biblical literalism, which rests upon the foundation of inerrancy, unlocks the mystery of the path of our actual salvation at the end of all things. This unassailable certainty that literalism provides insulates the believer from all of the evils the modern world offers.

It is certainly undeniable that literalism and premillennialism have played important roles in the formation and development of Christian fundamentalism, there are those who have suggested, however, that they must be regarded as secondary to the militancy with which fundamentalists describe themselves as at odds with secular culture. Biblical literalism and inerrancy may have led to a scriptural exegesis capable of providing a straightforward account of the creation of the world or how the world will end, but what most strongly identifies Christian fundamentalism, these cataloguers of fundamentalism offer, is the manner in which they understand themselves to be at war with the enemies of God's truth.

George Marsden, in his *Fundamentalism and American Culture*, recounts that following the early twentieth-century publication of *The Fundamentals*, fundamentalism became most identifiable with the call to save American civilization from the dangers of evolution.[66] That is, fundamen-

---

63. Sandeen, *The Roots of Fundamentalism*, 13, 233.
64. Boone, *The Bible Tells Them So*, 53.
65. Boone, *The Bible Tells Them So*, 109.
66. Marsden, *Fundamentalism and American Culture*, 141.

talism was born of the particular ideologies identified by others, but it was its commitment to fighting the culture wars that truly names the heart of Christian fundamentalism. In evidence of this, Marsden provides the fact that American Protestant fundamentalists constantly return to those Scripture passages that emphasize the warfare between the forces of good and evil. That they most often understand these verses spiritually and not advocating physical warfare does not change the fact that Christian fundamentalists describe themselves as engaged in a very real battle for the salvation of souls and the cause of goodness. Nancy Ammerman, another important voice on fundamentalism, in her "North American Protestant Fundamentalism," offers Tim LaHaye's 1980 book, *The Battle for the Mind* as an example of precisely this type of fundamentalist rhetoric.[67] Ammerman's discussion, however, predates another LaHaye contribution, this one notably with Jerry Jenkins, that famously built upon the notion of spiritual warfare blossoming into the apocalypse in the form of their bestselling *Left Behind* series.

Naming the defining characteristic of Christian fundamentalism is fraught with difficulties, most critically in our contemporary context. I contend, however, that the defining mark of the fundamentalist lies elsewhere. To find it, we must take a foray into the world of eighteenth-century Scottish philosophy.

Thomas Reid (1710–96), a Christian minister and professor at the University of Aberdeen, spent most of his career attempting to defend the beliefs and perspectives of the common person from the commitments of Early Modern philosophical thought, which assumed that the demands of reason were simply too sophisticated to allow anyone but the most intellectually elite to be trusted. The demanding philosophical systems of René Descartes, John Locke, George Berkeley, and others rendered the common person as experiencing a world far different from the one that actually existed. To make matters worse, the infamous skeptic David Hume demonstrated that, given the assumptions of their systems, the philosopher is also completely adrift in a world that they themselves can neither know nor understand.

Hume demonstrated that the philosophically reasonable starting point from which this school of philosophy, often referred to as empiricism, begins inescapably leads to a complete collapse of any and all systems of knowledge. The damming conclusion of Hume's thesis was that we have no justification for trusting our senses, theology, or science. These frightening ideas pale in comparison, however, to Hume's philosophical demonstration that we, in fact, are not justified to believe even in our own existence. In the face of such a despairing skepticism, Reid offered an inspired response.

---

67. Ammerman, "North American Protestant Fundamentalism," 40.

The "ideal system," the philosophical approach that Hume inherited from Descartes and Locke, Reid likened to a Trojan Horse, whose outward appearance is both beautiful and innocent, but which carries in her belly the "death and destruction" of all knowledge and common sense.[68] He argued that Hume rightly demonstrated that adherence to such a system ultimately annihilates notions of causation, time and space, body, and even soul, leaving us with nothing more than thoughts, sensations, and passions without persons.[69] For the empiricist to reject such a conclusion, Reid confessed, was inconceivable. To accept it, however, was absurd. The problem, Reid argued, lay in the acceptance of the empiricists' first principle, which Hume rendered, "[We] may divide all the perceptions of the mind into two classes or species which are distinguished by their different degrees of force and vivacity, . . . ideas [and] impressions."[70] Like a train of dominos whose end is already doomed to fall in the knocking over of the first, Reid saw in this first principle the downfall of all knowledge. Yet, as Hume went on to ask for philosophical defenses of persons, causation, and the external world, Reid offered that we should in turn demand a similar defense of the precepts of empiricism.[71] That is, if Hume called into question the trustworthiness of all reasoning, should we not hold this same skeptical position in regards to his reasoning concerning impressions and ideas, which brought us to this skeptical conclusion in the first place?[72]

To this question, Reid argued, Hume has no answer. He claimed that Hume further contradicts himself by believing, against his own principles, that his work should be read and his "metaphysical acumen" honored, despite his work and acumen being instances of precisely what he claimed quite simply cannot be trusted.[73] Rather than this skeptical system so fraught with inconsistencies, Reid argued, we should turn instead to the powers of common sense, which, even with all the theology and so-called "superstition" carried with it, still asks of us a lesser degree of trust. It was his contention that "this article of *sceptical creed* is indeed so full of mystery . . . it appears to require as much faith as that of St. Athanasius."[74] Our error lay, according to Reid, in looking to the philosopher for first principles. Rather, he encourages us to appeal to the common experience of the "vulgar." Reid concluded

---

68. Reid, *Essays on the Active Powers of the Human Mind*, 481.
69. Reid, *Essays on the Intellectual Powers of Man*, 301.
70. Hume, *An Enquiry Concerning Human Understanding*, 10.
71. Reid, *An Inquiry into the Human Mind on the Principles of Common Sense*, 376.
72. Reid, *Essays on the Intellectual Powers of Man*, 214.
73. Reid, *An Inquiry into the Human Mind on the Principles of Common Sense*, 409.
74. Reid, *An Inquiry into the Human Mind on the Principles of Common Sense*, 331.

that Hume has made precisely this error. It is from the vast fields of common sense that Hume's first principles should have been harvested; instead, Hume, in his pride, sought after that elusive quality of certainty from within the hallowed halls of the university, and so inherited their hubris. Having recognized the dangers of that system of knowledge, Reid then worked to replace it with one built upon the foundation of common sense.

He began his discussion with the assertion that the faculties of the human mind are no less trustworthy in achieving their ends as the organs of the human body.[75] That is, despite Hume's skeptical position, he never actually failed to believe that his hand would move his pen across the page properly to communicate his thoughts, that his eyes would be able to guide him towards the chair on which he sat while he wrote, nor that his ears would alert him to the presence of a visitor at the door even during his most intense speculation.[76]

Thus, in his own philosophical work, Reid began with an immediate departure from the *ideal system*. In that system, the mind passively receives pieces of sensory perception that the mind then attempts to puzzle together. This, Reid argued, is fiction. Rather, our senses encounter objects as they truly are, not in shattered slivers that I must then painstakingly piece together. I see a rose as a rose and not as a flood of impressions of color, extension, weight, smell, and feel that I then cobble together. The human experience, Reid concluded, is filled with observations of precisely this variety. Moreover, the arrogance of philosophers notwithstanding, the remainder of the human community regard these simple, unreflective experiences as perfectly useful and warranted exactly as they are:[77]

> I conclude, then, that the belief which accompanies sensation and memory, is a simple act of the mind, which cannot be defined. It is in this respect like seeing and hearing, which can never be so defined, as to be understood by those who have not these faculties; and to such as have them, no definition can make these operations more clear than they are already. In like manner, every man . . . knows perfectly well what belief is, but can never define or explain it.[78]

Any attempt, then, to analyze belief further is quite simply a muddying of the waters. One does not find themselves inundated with a myriad of perceptions that they must then turn into something sensible. Rather,

---

75. Reid, *An Inquiry into the Human Mind on the Principles of Common Sense*, 397.
76. Reid, *An Inquiry into the Human Mind on the Principles of Common Sense*, 20.
77. Wolterstorff, "Hume and Reid," 406.
78. Reid, *An Inquiry into the Human Mind on the Principles of Common Sense*, 30.

the moment of discovery as to what a thing is arises simultaneous with its initially being observed.[79] In other words, we do not experience brownness, largeness, flatness, smoothness, and tallness, etc., and then out of them construct the image of a table. It is only after seeing a table, immediately as a table, that one can analyze such an experience and break it down into its component parts. And furthermore, anyone who tries to claim otherwise is not only confused, but also stands against the weight of the whole of human experience.

In this, Reid became the champion of those types of knowledge for which Early Modern philosophy could not account. Despite Hume's conclusion that belief in God, miracles, souls, and saviors could never be justified, Reid provided a system of knowledge in which the Christian could be sure that their cherished faith touched Truth. The story of how this Reidien approach gets passed down to the Evangelicalism of the early twentieth century is much too involved for our purposes here. It is clear, however, that as Hume's approach blossomed into the system that bolstered the scientific and philosophical vision that so famously simply dismissed religious claims, the Reidian defense of common sense is what provided the Evangelical confidence to insist upon the inerrancy and literalism of the Scriptures in face of the attacks of liberalism. Becoming the dominant American philosophical perspective between the American Revolution and Civil War,[80] Reidian common sense philosophy entered most directly into mainstream Protestant academic circles through Princeton seminary's particularly strong allegiance to it.[81]

What this Reidian approach offered conservative Protestantism was the notion that there was justification for something being the case simply in virtue of the fact that it seemed to be the case. That is, viewing Scripture through the lens of a Reidian system of knowledge moved the onus of proof onto those who suggest that the meaning of Scripture is other than what it most readily appears to say. In such a perspective, then, certainty and surety were no longer exclusive to the intellectual elite in their ivory tower but returned to the common person.

---

79. Reid, *Essays on the Intellectual Powers of Man*, 106.

80. Noll, "Common Sense Traditions and American Evangelical Thought," 219. Noll demonstrates that common sense realism became the largely agreed upon philosophical background for Americans in general and Evangelicals in particular given its rejection of the assumptions that were so firmly bolstering the English perspectives. The acceptance of Scottish common sense philosophy is, thus, best understood as another feature of American revolution.

81. Fitzgerald, *The Evangelicals*, 75.

There is, however, a problem. Reid just quite simply misread Hume (in Reid's defense, so have very many others). The first section of Hume's *A Treatise of Human Nature*, which he entitled "Of Knowledge," concludes with a reflection on his philosophical journey thus far. He begins by confessing the fear and isolation of the position in which he has found himself.

> I call upon others to join me, in order to make a company apart; but no one will hearken to me. Every one keeps at a distance, and dreads that storm, which beats upon me from every side. I have expos'd myself to the enmity of all metaphysicians, logicians, mathematicians, and even theologians; and can I wonder at the insults I must suffer?[82]

It is clear then, that Hume recognizes the gravity of his contribution thus far and the skeptical conclusions he has reached. Insofar as he was levying a sustained critique against the Lockean system, Hume was successful. There is no denying that Hume has found himself at this point in a radically skeptical position. He saw himself isolated and alone, the enemy of philosophers and theologians alike. It is clear that Hume was not at all comfortable simply ending his investigation there. He wrote that he recognizes the absurdity of his position when so much of what he has demonstrated to be unknowable are precisely those ideas "which are common to human nature" and for which he feels strongly compelled to continue to hold despite his commitment to his previous discussion.[83] *Experience* of a world that appears to make sense and *habitually believing* it all to make sense, Hume confessed, are all that remain to explain his justification in all of those ideas "common to human nature." These two "flights of fancy," experience and habit, are our last defense from the total skepticism that has been steadily advancing toward us.[84] Poor as these notions might appear, for Hume, it turns out, they were enough.

Despite the absence of any philosophically defensible proof for all of the common assumptions with which we navigate our world, Hume found that he was "absolutely and necessarily determin'd to live, and talk, and act like other people in the common affairs of life."[85] In committing ourselves to the systems of knowledge inherited from Locke, we must conclude that reason cannot dispel these skeptical conclusions, yet, Hume rejoiced, "nature herself suffices to that purpose," curing us of our philosophical

---

82. Hume, *A Treatise of Human Nature*, 172.
83. Hume, *A Treatise of Human Nature*, 172.
84. Hume, *A Treatise of Human Nature*, 175.
85. Hume, *A Treatise of Human Nature*, 175.

melancholy.[86] Our philosophy must be tempered by the reality of our position in the world. In other words, as Hume offered, "Be a philosopher; but amidst your philosophy, be still a man."[87]

The Lockean error lay not in failing to reach Hume's skeptical conclusion, but rather in the absurdity of claiming to restrict one's philosophy to only those ideas that can be known with certainty. Locke claimed to be providing an account of the very foundation of our sensory experience, yet before he even began, he sat upon a chair to write more comfortably, brought with him a pen and paper to record his findings, and continued to eat and drink, assuming the very things he was setting out to prove. Hume demonstrated that the great sin of the philosophers lay in thinking that they could escape their position as human persons and write about the world as if exterior to it. The world that remains after the Lockean analysis is one that in no way resembles the world in which we actually live. To this end, Hume concluded, "Human Nature is the only science of man; and yet has been hitherto the most neglected."[88] Having come to this conclusion, he ended his discussion of the foundations of knowledge and turned to emotions and morality for the remainder of his investigation.

What difference does this all make for our purposes? It is simply this: Reid offered an account of that which is inherently complex as eminently simple and straightforward, while Hume accepted the limitations of human finitude and sought to understand the progress we can make in light of them.[89] That is, Reid sought to make philosophy common sense. Hume, on the other hand, recognized that common sense is all that we have that we can truly call philosophy. Reid thinks he fixed this problem. Hume demonstrated that we would never be able to escape it and aided us in wrestling with it as best we can. And this, I offer, is central to every form of fundamentalism.

Fundamentalism takes on a variety of different forms and, thus, is often difficult to recognize, even more so now that the term is most commonly rejected by those who once accepted the name. Currently, we tend to use

---

86. Hume, *A Treatise of Human Nature*, 175.
87. Hume, *An Enquiry Concerning Human Understanding*, 4.
88. Hume, *A Treatise of Human Nature*, 177.

89. I certainly do not want to make light of the nontraditional reading of David Hume that I am offering, and I have elsewhere (in my second Master's thesis) explored these ideas more fully. In the interests of both space and focus, I would like to offer for now the relatively recent school of Humean exegesis referred to as the New Hume found in, e.g., Read and Richman, eds., *The New Hume Debate*; Strawson, *The Secret Connexion*; and Wright, *The Sceptical Realism of David Hume*. This same approach is expertly applied to Hume's account of morality in MacIntyre, "Hume on 'Is' and 'Ought.'"

this label to describe those whose views appear only at the fringes of society. We are most comfortable applying this description to, for instance, radical Islamic jihadists or the funeral-protesting members of Westboro Baptist Church. If we look at what both of these (and many other) groups share, despite their incredible differences, we find *an absolute and unshakeable certainty in their beliefs*. For Westboro Baptist, they understand themselves as the only remaining remnant of the New Testament church and, thus, the only contemporary group that accurately understands and lives out God's commands.[90] In defense of the host of bizarre positions they hold, Shirley Phelps-Roper, daughter of Westboro Baptist Church founder, Fred Phelps, explains that Westboro's approach is "not rocket science!" and that such a perspective is available to all who would employ a common-sense interpretation of the Scriptures.[91]

This unshakeable confidence in the certainty of their own perspectives is equally as present in the pages of Richard Dawkins' *The God Delusion* as is in the halls of The Creation Museum. While different in so many other ways, both Dawkins and The Creation Museum's parent organization, Answers in Genesis, hold their positions to be a matter of common sense and entirely unassailable. Moreover, both Dawkins and The Creation Museum have nothing to learn from those with whom they disagree.

When coming from the mouths of Christians, however, such certainty appears more familiar. These Christian fundamentalists sound like and often see themselves in the lineage of Jonathan Edward's "Sinner's in the Hands of an Angry God." As Frances Fitzgerald explains in her *The Evangelicals: The Struggle to Shape America*, there is in fact a massive difference between them. For the Christian fundamentalists of our day, as for Jonathan Edwards, sin is the cause of the degradation of society. Yet, for Edwards, it was *our* sinfulness that was causing such societal suffering and immorality.[92] This new message from late twentieth- and now early twenty-first-century fundamentalism claims that "sin lay not in the souls of [the] congregation, but in outside forces."[93] In Jonathan Edwards, as in John Paul II, the sinfulness poisoning society is, first, our own.

It is because of the legacy of Thomas Reid and the commonalities of a range of different forms of fundamentalism that I argue that the distinguishing mark of fundamentalism, born of an unshakeable confidence in a common-sense approach to knowledge, is certainty. Certainty is the ability

90. Barrett-Fox, *God Hates*, 43.
91. Barrett-Fox, *God Hates*, 27.
92. Fitzgerald, *The Evangelicals*, 308.
93. Fitzgerald, *The Evangelicals*, 308.

to *own* knowledge. It is the claim of *complete mastery* over at least a field of knowledge and, thus, the confidence to employ this knowledge perfectly in every context. It is, most disturbingly, the belief that the other can have nothing to offer because the fullness of knowledge and truth resides inside of those on the sides of the angels, which, most often, is "me" and "those that look, act, and live like me."

Returning to Hahn and the contributions of his *The First Society: The Sacrament of Matrimony and the Restoration of Social Order*, an important aspect of this work that we have not discussed thus far is the incredible range of complex issues that Hahn explains and answers in 182 pages! In this work, Hahn deals with notions of gender norms,[94] sexuality,[95] sacramentality,[96] economics,[97] Catholic philosophical commitments,[98] historical understandings of marriage,[99] abortion,[100] contraception,[101] ecclesiology,[102] liberalism,[103] biblical exegesis,[104] Old Testament legal categories,[105] western moral shift and degradation,[106] Marxism,[107] capitalism,[108] Catholic social teaching,[109] libertarianism,[110] Church and State,[111] fertility,[112] polygamy, homosexuality, self-marriage,[113] divorce,[114] and more. This is an incredible breadth of topics on which Hahn offers very definitive conclusions. And yet, given the wide range and critical importance of the topics he covers, in those

---

94. Hahn, *The First Society*, 10, 17.
95. Hahn, *The First Society*, 32, 90–91.
96. Hahn, *The First Society*, 161–74.
97. Hahn, *The First Society*, 69–70, 153.
98. Hahn, *The First Society*, 161.
99. Hahn, *The First Society*, 38–61.
100. Hahn, *The First Society*, 151.
101. Hahn, *The First Society*, 89–90.
102. Hahn, *The First Society*, 149–60.
103. Hahn, *The First Society*, xviii, 32–36, 103, 113.
104. Hahn, *The First Society*, 13–17, 51–61.
105. Hahn, *The First Society*, 21–22.
106. Hahn, *The First Society*, 25–50, 123–25.
107. Hahn, *The First Society*, 79.
108. Hahn, *The First Society*, 34, 155.
109. Hahn, *The First Society*, 83.
110. Hahn, *The First Society*, 96.
111. Hahn, *The First Society*, 96–98, 130–34.
112. Hahn, *The First Society*, 102.
113. Hahn, *The First Society*, 124.
114. Hahn, *The First Society*, 152.

182 pages, Hahn provides only nineteen footnotes, several of which are to his own books. Comparatively, Pope John Paul II's *Ecclesia in America*, the apostolic exhortation explored in the introduction to this discussion, provides 295 footnotes in a short 135 pages. Hahn's claims demand some kind of evidence. The weight of statements of the sort, "The Western world has spent much of the last few centuries trying to find or form a replacement for the unifying catholicity of the Catholic Church,"[115] and "in Western history, marriage and family have never been unrecognizable—until, perhaps, this moment, when even the most enduring conventions, such as the necessity of opposite-sex couples, are being dismissed,"[116] are claims that quite simply cannot stand on their own.

Yet, for Hahn, the world of theological, moral, social, and political truths is simply a matter of common sense. In answer to the question of how we fix a society that has been gutted of its very substance, he offers, "The solution, *of course*, is a reemergence of a robust culture of marriage"[117] and that marriage is "the key to everything we want to build in our society and culture."[118] He positions the family as "an interpretive *key that is available for everyone*" for understanding society.[119] And in concluding that the sacraments should be the center of all human communities given that they are essential to eternal life, Hahn states, "It doesn't get much simpler than that."[120] The answers, for Hahn, are simple and straightforward. This despite the fact that his approach is widely different, both in tone and content, than that offered by John Paul II discussed above. That is, if the answers are so simple, why does John Paul II not come to those same conclusions in *Ecclesia in America*?

It is not, however, just the solutions that are simple. In regards to the problems that we actually face, Hahn claims, "*All agree*, though, that we have squandered our civilizational patrimony, frittering away the treasury of Christian culture accumulated through the centuries on such ill-conceived vanity projects as the sexual revolution and relativistic mass consumerism."[121] When providing his understanding of the sacraments and their role in our salvation, Hahn simply states, "*Everyone agrees* that believing these truths is essential to the Catholic faith."[122] Moreover, the simplicity

---

115. Hahn, *The First Society*, 156.
116. Hahn, *The First Society*, 66.
117. Hahn, *The First Society*, 38, emphasis added.
118. Hahn, *The First Society*, xv.
119. Hahn, *The First Society*, 83, emphasis added.
120. Hahn, *The First Society*, 166.
121. Hahn, *The First Society*, xviii, emphasis added.
122. Hahn, *The First Society*, 131, emphasis added.

of these truths force us to recognize that the world outside of Catholicism has nothing to teach us:

> What this means is that, as Catholics we can't play ball with secularists with regard to the language of marriage. Just because the powers-that-be in our country have no idea what "sacramentality" is and couldn't tell the New Covenant from the New Deal doesn't mean that they are not subject to the truths of sacramentality and the New Covenant.[123]

Remembering that Hahn has argued that marriage is the answer to society's ills, it is hard to imagine that by "the language of marriage" Hahn is not including the entirety of Catholic social and moral teaching. After all, Hahn argues, "There is no neutrality between good and evil—not for us, and not for the state."[124] It is in this regard that *The First Society* departs from a discourse concerning Catholic Social Teaching and instead offers simply another overly narrow attempt at United States socio-political culture-war rhetoric.[125]

The vision that Hahn offers in *The First Society*, which he defines as the "implications of the truth of marriage for society and the state,"[126] is one in which the division of the world into easily recognizable spheres of good (Catholicism) and evil (everything else). The truth is simple and straightforward, but sin and pride in the guise of secularism, liberalism, and individualism prevent society from grasping it. And while Catholics might sometimes fail in their duties to the truth, the Church itself is the complete manifestation on earth of the heavenly reality of God's absolute perfection.[127]

Further evidence of Hahn's commitment to the perfection and completeness of the Catholic Church is the fact that in the entirety of this discussion of the collapse and restoration of society published in 2018, there

---

123. Hahn, *The First Society*, 129.
124. Hahn, *The First Society*, 98.
125. For a thorough explication of the religious right's engagement in moral and political culture war discourse, see James Davison Hunter's *Is There a Culture War?* and *Culture Wars* as well as Andrew Hartman's *A War for the Soul of America*. Matthew Sutton's *American Apocalypse*, Paul Boyer's *When Time Shall Be No More*, and Timothy Weber's *On the Road to Armageddon* all provided excellent analyses of the premillennialist roots and influence on current culture-war discourse. While discussion of culture war-ideology is largely restricted to engagement with the religious right, Jack Jenkins' recent *American Prophets* is an inspired discussion of the religious left's historical rejoinder to conservative social-political influence.
126. Hahn, *The First Society*, 23.
127. Hahn, *The First Society*, 164.

THE FUNDAMENTALS OF A TRULY CATHOLIC AMERICA   109

is not a single mention of the Catholic priest abuse crisis, nor the failing of the Church to confess and act appropriately in response to it. How can any contemporary Catholic writing on the troubled and difficult predicament of modern society fail to mention the role that the Church has played throughout the last century in furthering and, in places, even creating it? Apparently, the abuse of thousands upon thousands of innocent victims by those most responsible for guiding us to the sacraments and teaching us holiness has no bearing whatsoever in addressing the problems plaguing our society.

The priest abuse scandal is not, however, the only surprising omission here. Interestingly, despite his being elevated to the papacy in March of 2013, Pope Francis, a figure often erroneously associated in public discourse with American-style progressive ideology, is entirely absent from Hahn's discussion.[128] Moreover, this insulation from the recognition of our own culpability in creating the society in which we live Hahn also grants to himself. In his discussion of our culture's impotence as a result of our refusal to commit ourselves to the truth of the sacrament of marriage, Hahn makes only a single reference to his own marriage:

> But let's bring this down to earth: living together is hard. Habits and preferences clash; hidden tendencies and peccadillos are revealed; vices are magnified under the constant gaze of another person. I assiduously roll up the toothpaste; Kimberly does not. You can imagine the tension this causes.[129]

Even in offering the most insignificant of marital disagreements, Hahn cannot present himself as lacking.

The vision that Hahn offers, here and in the many other of his intellectual and social contributions, is one of common sense and certainty. Like Reid, he attempts to make the inherently complex simple, straightforward, and certain. And like every other fundamentalist, the problem lies with everyone else. It is in no way the fault of the Church in the abuse crisis that society has become what it is. It is not even Hahn's "hidden tendencies and peccadillos" that are worth confessing in an account of the monumental difficulty of marriage. After all, Kimberly is the one who fails to roll up the toothpaste. The truth, which Hahn offers without the need of external

---

128. In fact, it takes turning to Hahn's social media presence to find even the suggestion of his position on Francis' papacy. While never directly criticizing Pope Francis himself, Hahn, on several occasions, has shared to his thousands of friends and followers articles, written by others, critical of Francis or questioning his legitimacy. For examples, see Hahn's Facebook posts on August 18, 2018, August 26, 2018, August 27, 2018, August 30, 2018, September 4, 2018.

129. Hahn, *The First Society*, 144.

support or evidence in the form of appropriate footnotes, is simple and Hahn is one of its protectors. As discussed previously:

> I want to make clear that this idea—the idea behind this book—is nothing new, and it's certainly not mine. It's as old as the Church, and the Church has never let go of it, though the idea has been lost in the shuffle of doctrinal controversies over the last several centuries.[130]

Certainty born of common sense is the mark of Protestant fundamentalism. In this regard, Scott Hahn fits the definition of a fundamentalist. More than this, Scott Hahn fits all of the other significant markers of Protestant fundamentalism. Hahn defends in *Covenant and Communion*, his account of Benedict XVI's theology, a biblical inerrancy that matches fundamentalist understandings of inerrancy. He argues in *The Lamb's Supper* that the Mass acts as a key that we can use to unlock the eschatological vision of the book of Revelation, revealing the realities of spiritual warfare and possibly depicting the end of the world itself. He argues in *The First Society* that the Church Militant can have no peace with secularism and non-Catholic worldviews. Despite the almost complete dismissal by the Catholic academy as either unimportant or harmless, Scott Hahn—one of the most visible, prolific, successful, and influential voices in the Catholic Church in the United States—presents a thoroughly *fundamentalist* ideology. While a fundamentalism dressed in the robes of Catholicism, it is, nevertheless, identical in form and function to that which plagues the Protestant world. Moreover, his fundamentalist vision, which is not only read by but actively distributed widely among the Catholic laity in the United States and beyond, is one that, like its Protestant sibling, positions the problems we face in the world as always entirely the fault of the *Other*.

Gilbert Keith Chesterton (1874-1936), one of Catholicism's most cherished and prolific writers of recent history, was neither a priest nor a trained theologian. He is remembered as an accomplished author and public intellectual, whose wit, charm, and intellect endeared him to friends and critics alike. Chesterton's legacy is enshrined today mostly in regards to his *Orthodoxy*, an ingenious and often bizarre blend of religious autobiography, theology, philosophy, and humor, and *Heretics*, a flamboyant and incisive dismantling of aspects of liberalism that had become so prominent in his day as well as its most vocal defenders. Yet, during his life he was most well-known as a journalist and something of a public intellectual.

---

130. Hahn, *The Lamb's Supper*, 116.

A regular contributor to newspapers in his London hometown, Chesterton garnered acclaim for his singular style in his columns, which ranged from defense and interpretation of the exceptional nature of ordinary things to intensely pointed political and social commentary.[131] While publishing sixty-nine books during his incredible career, he gained a reputation during his life for his engagement with public intellectual discourse and debate. As compelling as Chesterton was during his public debates, it was his jovial nature and boisterous mirth that made Chesterton so memorable. He crossed swords with the intellectual elite of his day, most significantly with the famous George Bernard Shaw, and when, in the heat of debate, his opponents' critiques became jabs about his significant weight or personal failings, it was his own booming laugh that was loudest in the room.

His contributions were celebrated (and critiqued) for their profound simplicity and their reach to the common person, many for whom Chesterton became a guide and mentor. Among the many who attribute to Chesterton their own spiritual development and even conversion, the great Christian philosopher and theologian C. S. Lewis cites his initiation into Chesterton with the catalyst of his becoming Christian.

There is a very real sense in which G. K. Chesterton was one of *the* Catholic voices of his time, and his genius and contributions have remained with us even today. And when the *London Times* asked for a number of prominent writers and academics to respond with an essay to the question, "What's Wrong with the World?" he responded very simply, yet profoundly,

"Dear Sirs: I am."

Amen.

---

131. Wills, *Chesterton*, 69.

Bibliography

Ammerman, Nancy. "North American Protestant Fundamentalism." In *Fundamentalism Observed: The Fundamentalism Project*, edited by Scott Appleby and Martin Marty, Vol. 1, 1–65. Chicago: University of Chicago Press, 1991.
Aquinas, Thomas. *Rationibus Fidei*. Translated by Joseph Kenny, O.P. Accessed January 3, 2020. http://dhspriory.org/thomas/Rationes.htm.
———. *Summa Theologiae*. Translated by Alfred Freddoso. Accessed March 5, 2019. https://www3.nd.edu/~afreddos/summa-translation/TOC.htm.
Asiedu, F. B. A. "The Song of Songs and the Ascent of the Soul: Ambrose, Augustine, and the Language of Mysticism." *Vigiliae Christianae* 55.3 (2001) 299–317.
Augustine. *The Confessions of Saint Augustine*. Translated by Philip Burton. New York: Knopf, 2001.
Barber, Michael Patrick. "Jesus as the Davidic Temple Builder and Peter's Priestly Role in Matthew 16–19." *Journal of Biblical Literature* 132.4 (2013) 935–53.
Barrett-Fox, Rebecca. *God Hates: Westboro Baptist Church, American Nationalism, and the Religious Right*. Lawrence, KS: University Press of Kansas, 2016.
Barth, Karl, and Joseph Ratzinger. *Revelations and Tradition*. New York: Herder and Herder, 1966.
Benedict XVI. *Church Fathers: From Clement to Augustine*. Translated by L'Osservatore Romano. San Francisco: Ignatius, 2008.
———. "Declaratio," Speeches. February 10, 2013, at the Vatican. http://w2.vatican.va/content/benedict-xvi/en/speeches/2013/february/documents/hf_ben-xvi_spe_20130211_declaratio.html.
Biguzzi, Giancarlo. "Is the Babylon of Revelation Rome or Jerusalem." *Biblica* 87.3 (2006) 371–86.
Boeve, Lieven, "Introduction." In *The Ratzinger Reader: Mapping a Theological Journey*, edited by Lieven Boeve and Gerard Mannion, 1–12. London: T. & T. Clark, 2010.
———. "Theological Foundation: Revelation, Tradition, and Hermeneutics." In *The Ratzinger Reader: Mapping a Theological Journey*, edited by Lieven Boeve and Gerard Mannion, 13–50. London: T. & T. Clark International, 2010.
Boone, Kathleen. *The Bible Tells Them So: The Discourse of Protestant Fundamentalism*. Albany, NY: State University of New York Press, 1989.
Bouyer, Louis. *Newman: His Life and Spirituality—An Intellectual and Spiritual Biography of John Henry Newman*. San Francisco: Ignatius, 2011.
Boyer, Paul. *When Time Shall Be No More: Prophecy Belief in Modern American Culture*. Cambridge: Bellknap, 1992.

Brown, Michael Joseph. "Paul's Use of ΔΟΥΛΟΣ ΧΡΙΣΤΟΥ ΙΗΣΟΥ in Romans 1:1." *Journal of Biblical Literature* 120.4 (2001) 723–37.
Brown, Raymond. *An Introduction to the New Testament: The Abridged Edition*. Edited by Marion L. Soards. New Haven, CT: Yale University Press, 2016.
———. "Pater Noster and Escahatological Prayer." *Theological Studies* 22 (1961) 175–208.
Burger, Hans, Arnold Huijgen, and Eroc Peels, eds. *Sola Scriptura: Biblical and Theological Perspectives on Scripture, Authority, and Hermeneutics*. Leiden: Brill, 2018.
Catechism of the Catholic Church. 2nd ed. Washington, DC: United States Catholic Conference, 2000.
Collins, John J. *The Apocalyptic Imagination: An Introduction to Jewish Apocalyptic Literature*. 3rd ed. Grand Rapids: Eerdmans, 2016.
Cunningham, Lawrence S. "John Henry Newman: The Challenge to Evangelical Religion." *Horizons* 30.1 (2003) 144–46.
Dahlberg, Bruce T. "The Typological Use of Jeremiah 1:4–19 in Matthew 16:13–23." *Journal of Biblical Literature* 94.1 (1975) 73–80.
Daniélou, "Sacraments and Parousia." *Orates Fratres* 25 (1950/51) 400–404.
Deissman, Adolf. *Light from the Ancient East*. Translated by Lionel Strachan. New York: Aeterna, 2015.
Derrida, Jacques. *Of Grammatology*. Translated by Gayatri Chakavorty Spivak. Baltimore: John's Hopkins University Press, 1974.
———. "Unsealing (the Old Language)." In *Points... Interviews*, translated by P. Kamuf et al., edited by E. Weber, 115–31. Stanford, CA: Stanford University Press, 1995.
Dobell, Brian. *Augustine's Intellectual Conversion: The Journey from Platonism to Christianity*. Cambridge: Cambridge University Press, 2009.
Farrer, Austin. *A Rebirth in Images: The Making of St. John's Apocalypse*. Westminster, UK: Dacre, 1949.
Favro, Diane. "'Pater urbis': Augustius as City Father of Rome." *Journal of the Society of Architectural Historians* 51.5 (1992) 61–84.
Fitzgerald, Frances. *The Evangelicals: The Struggle to Shape America*. New York: Simon and Schuster, 2017.
Francis. *Let Us Dream: The Path to a Better Future*. New York: Simon and Schuster, 2020.
Gadenz, Pablo. "Magisterial Teaching on the Inspiration and Truth of Scripture: Precedents and Prospects." *For the Sake of Our Salvation: The Truth and Humility of God's Word. Letter & Spirit* 6 (2010) 67–92.
Gourlay, Thomas. "The Nuptial Character of the Relationship between Faith and Reason in the Thought of Joseph Ratzinger/Benedict XVI." *The Heythrop Journal* 59 (2018) 265–72.
Greisz, Germain. "The Inspiration and Inerrancy of Scripture." *For the Sake of Our Salvation: The Truth and Humility of God's Word. Letter & Spirit* 6 (2010) 181–90.
Hahn, Scott. *Consuming the Word: The New Testament and the Eucharist in the Early Church*. New York: Image, 2013.
———. *Covenant and Communion: The Biblical Theology of Pope Benedict XVI*. Grand Rapids: Brazos, 2009.
———. *The Creed: Professing the Faith through the Ages*. Steubenville, OH: Emmaus Road, 2016.

———. "Introduction." *For the Sake of Our Salvation: The Truth and Humility of God's Word. Letter & Spirit* 6 (2010) 11–20.

———. *The First Society: The Sacrament of Marriage and the Restoration of the Social Order*. Steubenville, OH: Emmaus Road, 2018.

———. "For the Sake of Our Salvation: The Truth and Humility of God's Word. *For the Sake of Our Salvation: The Truth and Humility of God's Word. Letter & Spirit* 6 (2010) 21–46.

———. *The Fourth Cup: Unveiling the Mystery of the Last Supper and the Cross*. New York: Crown, 2018.

———. *The Lamb's Supper: The Mass as Heaven on Earth*. New York: Doubleday, 1999.

———. *Letter and Spirit: From Written Text to Living Word in the Liturgy*. New York: Doubleday, 2005.

———. *Reasons to Believe: How to Understand, Explain, and Defend the Catholic Faith*. New York: Doubleday, 2007.

———. *Rome Sweet Home: Our Journey to Catholicism*. San Francisco: Ignatius, 1993.

———. "The Scott Hahn Conversion Story." Accessed December 12, 2019. https://www.catholiceducation.org/en/religion-and-philosophy/apologetics/the-scott-hahn-conversion-story.html.

Hahn, Scott, and Curtis Mitch. "Introduction to the Ignatius Catholic Study Bible." *Ignatius Catholic Study Bible*. San Francisco: Ignatius, 2001.

Hartman, Andrew. *A War for the Soul of America: A History of the Culture Wars*. Chicago: The University of Chicago Press, 2015.

Hentschel, Jason. "Evangelicals and the Quest for Certainty: Making Sense of Our Battles for the Bible." PhD diss., University of Dayton, 2015, accessed April 5, 2020. http://rave.ohiolink.edu/etdc/view?acc_num=dayton1446479845.

Hume, David. *An Enquiry Concerning Human Understanding*. Edited by Eric Steinberg. Indianapolis: Hackett, 1977.

———. *A Treatise of Human Nature*. Oxford: Oxford University Press, 2000.

Hunter, James Davison. *Culture Wars: The Struggle to Define America*. New York: Basic, 1991.

Hunter, James Davison, and Alan Wolfe. *Is There a Culture War? A Dialogue on Values and American Public Life*. Washington, DC: Brookings Institute Press, 2006.

Jenkins, Jack. *American Prophets: The Religious Roots of Progressive Politics and the Ongoing Fight for the Soul of the Country*. New York: HarperCollins, 2020.

John Paul II. *Ecclesia in America*. Apostolic Exhortation on the Church in America. January 22, 1999; at Mexico City. Washington, DC: United States Catholic Conference, 1999.

———. *Redemptoris Mater*. Encyclical on the Blessed Virgin Mary. March 25, 1987; at the Holy See. http://www.vatican.va/content/john-paul-ii/en/encyclicals/documents/hf_jp-ii_enc_25031987_redemptoris-mater.html.

Josephus. *The Jewish War*. Translated by J. Thackery. In *Josephus*, Vol. 3, edited by E. Page, 2–634. Cambridge: Harvard University Press, 1961.

Kingsbury, Jack Dean. "The Figure of Peter in Matthew's Gospel as a Theological Problem." *Journal of Biblical Literature* 98.1 (1979) 67–83.

Koester, Craig R. "On the Verge of the Millennium: A History of the Interpretation of Revelation," *Word & World* XV.2 (1995) 128–36.

Leo XIII. *Aeterni Patris*. Encyclical on the Restoration of Christian Philosophy. August 4, 1879; at the Holy See. http://www.vatican.va/content/leo-xiii/en/encyclicals/documents/hf_l-xiii_enc_04081879_aeterni-patris.html.

———. *Providentissimus Deus*. Encyclical on the Study of Holy Scripture. November 18, 1893. http://www.vatican.va/content/leo-xiii/en/encyclicals/documents/hf_l-xiii_enc_18111893_providentissimus-deus.html.

Levering, Matthew. "The Inspiration of Scripture: A *Status Quaestionis*." *For the Sake of Our Salvation: The Truth and Humility of God's Word. Letter & Spirit* 6 (2010) 281–314.

MacIntyre, Alasdair. "Hume on 'Is' and 'Ought.'" *The Philosophical Review* 68.4 (1959) 451–68.

Mannion, Gerard. "Liturgy, Catechesis, and Evangelization." In *The Ratzinger Reader*, edited by Lieven Boeve and Gerard Mannion, 225–56. London: T. & T. Clark, 2010.

Marsden, George. *Fundamentalism and American Culture*. Oxford: Oxford University Press, 2006.

Martyr, Justin. *First Apology*. Translated by Marcus Dods and George Reith. In *Ante-Nicene Christian Library: Translation of the Writings of the Fathers Down to A.D. 325*. Edinburgh: T. & T. Clark, 1872.

Merton, Thomas. "Liturgy and Spiritual Personalism." *Worship* 34.9 (1960) 494–507.

Mills, D. Forrest. "Augustine's Conversion in his Confessions 8: Some Disputed Issues." *The Evangelical Quarterly* 90.4 (2019) 326–41.

Morrow, Jeffrey. "The Modernist Crisis and the Shifting of Catholic Views on Biblical Inspiration." *For the Sake of Our Salvation: The Truth and Humility of God's Word. Letter & Spirit* 6 (2010) 265–80.

Nauta, Rein. "The Prodigal Son: Some Psychological Aspects of Augustine's Conversion to Christianity." *Journal of Religious Health* 47.1 (2008) 75–88.

Newman, John Henry. *Apologia Pro Vita Sua*. London: Penguin, 2004.

———. *An Essay on the Development of Doctrine*. Notre Dame, IN: University of Notre Dame Press, 1989.

Noll, Mark. "Common Sense Traditions and American Evangelical Thought." *American Quarterly* 37.2 (1985) 216–38.

Oakes, Edward T., S.J. "Resolving the Relativity Paradox: Pope Benedict and the Challenge of Christological Relativism." In *Explorations in the Theology of Benedict XVI*, edited by John Cavadini, 87–113. Notre Dame, IN: University of Notre Dame Press, 2012.

O'Connell, Robert, J., S.J. *Images of Conversion in St. Augustine's Confessions*. New York: Fordham University Press, 1996.

———. *Soundings in St. Augustine's Imagination*. New York: Fordham University Press, 1994.

O'Malley, John W. "Does Church Teaching Change? Church Doctrine at Trent, Vatican I, and Vatican II." *Commonweal*, July 31, 2019. https://www.commonwealmagazine.org/does-church-teaching-change.

O'Regan, Cyril. "Benedict the Augustinian." In *Explorations in the Theology of Benedict XVI*, edited by John C. Cavadini, 21–62. Notre Dame, IN: Notre Dame University Press, 2012.

Parry, Ken. "The Nature and Scope of Patristics." *The Wiley Blackwell Companion to Patristics*, edited by Ken Parry, 1–11. Oxford: Wiley and Sons, 2015.

Paul VI. *Dei Verbum*. Dogmatic Constitution on Divine Revelation. November 18, 1965; at the Holy See. http://www.vatican.va/archive/hist_councils/ii_vatican_council/documents/vat-ii_const_19651118_dei-verbum_en.html.
———. *Humanae Vitae*. Encyclical Letter on the Regulation of Birth. July 25, 1968; at the Holy See. http://www.vatican.va/content/paul-vi/en/encyclicals/documents/hf_p-vi_enc_25071968_humanae-vitae.html.
Peckham, John. "Sola Scriptura: Reductio Ad Absurdum," *Trinity Journal* 35.2 (2014) 195–223.
Pitre, Brant. "The Mystery of God's Word: Inspiration, Inerrancy, and the Interpretation of Scripture." *For the Sake of Our Salvation: The Truth and Humility of God's Word. Letter & Spirit* 6 (2010) 47–66.
Pius X. *Pascendi Dominici Gregis*. On the Doctrines of the Modernists. September 8, 1907; at the Holy See. http://www.vatican.va/content/pius-x/en/encyclicals/documents/hf_p-x_enc_19070908_pascendi-dominici-gregis.html.
Pius XI. *Casti Connubii*. Encyclical on Christian Marriage. December 31, 1930; at the Holy See. http://www.vatican.va/content/pius-xi/en/encyclicals/documents/hf_p-xi_enc_19301231_casti-connubii.html.
Pius XII. *Divino Afflante Spiritu*. Encyclical Promoting Biblical Studies. September 30, 1943; at the Holy See. http://www.vatican.va/content/pius-xii/en/encyclicals/documents/hf_p-xii_enc_30091943_divino-afflante-spiritu.html.
———. *Summi Pontificatus*. Encyclical on the Unity of Human Society. October 20, 1939; at Castel Gandolfo. http://www.vatican.va/content/pius-xii/en/encyclicals/documents/hf_p-xii_enc_20101939_summi-pontificatus.html.
Pontifical Biblical Commission. *The Inspiration and Truth of Sacred Scripture: The Word That Comes from God and Speaks of God for the Salvation of the World*. Collegeville, MN: Liturgical, 2014.
———. "The Interpretation of the Bible in the Church." Presented to Pope John Paul II on April 23, 1993; https://catholic-resources.org/ChurchDocs/PBC_Interp-FullText.htm.
Ratzinger, Joseph. "Biblical Interpretation in Crisis: On the Question of the Foundations and Approaches of Exegesis Today." In *The Essential Pope Benedict*, edited by John F. Thornton and Susan B. Varenne, 243–58. New York: HarperCollins, 2007.
———. "Crisis in Catechesis." *Canadian Catholic Review* 7 (1983) 7–9.
———. "Homily at the Mass for the Election of the Roman Pontiff." April 18, 2005. In *The Essential Pope Benedict XVI: His Central Writings and Speeches*, edited by F. Thornton and Susan B. Varenne, 21–24. New York: HarperSanFrancisco, 2007.
———. *Jesus of Nazareth: From the Baptism in the Jordan*, Vol. 1. Translated by Adrian J. Walker. New York: Doubleday Broadway, 2007.
———. *A New Song for the Lord*. New York: Herder and Herder, 1996.
———. *Principles of Catholic Theology: Building Stones for a Fundamental Theology*. Translated by Sister Mary Frances McCarthy, SND. San Francisco: Ignatius, 1987.
———. "Relationship between Magisterium and Exegetes." Address to Pontifical Biblical Commission, *L'Osservatore Romano*, July 23, 2003.
———. "What Is Theology?" In *Principles of Catholic Thought: Building Stones for a Fundamental Theology*, 315–21. San Francisco: Ignatius, 1987.
Read, Rupert, and Kenneth Richman. *The New Hume Debate*. Rev. ed. London: Routledge, 2000.

Reid, Thomas. *Essays on the Intellectual Powers of Man. The Works of Thomas Reid: Vol. 2.* Boston: Adamant Media Corporation, 2000.

———. *An Inquiry into the Human Mind on the Principle of Common Sense.* Whitefish, MT: Kessinger, 2005.

Rowland, Tracey. "The World in the Theology of Joseph Ratzinger/Benedict XVI." *Journal of Moral Theology* 2.2 (2013) 109–32.

Sacred Congregation for the Doctrine of the Faith. "Faith and Demonology." *L'Osservatore Romano*, English Edition, July 10, 1975, 6–10.

Saller, Richard. "Pater Familias, Mater Familias, and the Gendered Semantics of the Roman Household." *Classical Philology* 94.2 (1999) 182–97.

Sandeen, Ernest. *The Roots of Christian Fundamentalism: British and American Millenarianism 1800–1930.* Chicago: The University of Chicago Press, 1970.

Short, Edward. *Newman and His Family.* London: Bloomsbury, 2013.

St. Paul Center. "About the Center." St. Paul Center. Accessed December 31, 2019. https://stpaulcenter.com/about/.

———. "Fellows." St. Paul Center. Accessed December 31, 2019. https://stpaulcenter.com/academic-projects/fellows/.

———. "Home Page." St. Paul Center. Accessed December 31, 2019. https://stpaulcenter.com/

Strawson, Galen. *The Secret Connexion: Causation, Realism, and David Hume.* Oxford: Oxford University Press, 2014.

Sutton, Matthew Avery. *American Apocalypse: A History of Modern Evangelicalism.* Cambridge: Bellknap, 2017.

Thucydides. *The Peloponnesian War.* Translated by Martin Hammond. Accessed March 5, 2019. http://data.perseus.org/citations/urn:cts:greekLit:tlg0003.tlg001.perseus-eng1:1.128.

Trollinger, Susan, and V. William, Jr. *Righting America at the Creation Museum.* Baltimore: Johns Hopkins University Press, 2016.

Turner, Frank. *John Henry Newman: The Challenge to Evangelical Religion.* New Haven, CT: Yale University Press, 2002.

United States Conference of Catholic Bishops. "The Book of Revelation." Accessed March 5, 2019. http://www.usccb.org/bible/revelation/0.

Van den Berg, Jacob, ed. *In Search of Truth : Augustine, Manichaeism and Other Gnosticism. Studies for Johannes Van Oort at Sixty.* Nag Hammadi and Manichaean Studies V. 74. Leiden: Brill, 2011.

The Vatican. "Biography of His Holiness, Pope Benedict XVI." Benedict XVI. Accessed April 5, 2020. https://w2.vatican.va/content/benedict-xvi/en/biography/documents/hf_ben-xvi_bio_20050419_short-biography_old.html

Von Hildebrand, Dietrich. *Transformation in Christ: On Christian Attitude.* San Francisco: Ignatius, 2001.

Walsh, Sr. Mary Ann. "The Life and Ministry of Saint. John Paul II." USCCB.org. Accessed February 23, 2020. http://www.usccb.org/about/leadership/holy-see/john-paul-ii/index.cfm.

Weber, Timothy P. *On the Road to Armageddon: How Evangelicals Became Israel's Best Friend.* Ada, MI: Baker Academic, 2005.

Wiley, Daniel P. "Tradition and Sola Scriptura in 2 Thessalonians 2:15." *Bibliotheca Sacra* 175.699 (2018) 323–37.

Wills, Gary. *Chesterton.* Rev. ed. New York: Image, 2001.

———. *Saint Augustine's Conversion*. New York: Viking, 2004.
Wolterstorff, Nicholas. "Hume and Reid." *The Monist* 70.4 (1987) 398–417.
Wright, John P. *The Sceptical Realism of David Hume*. Manchester, UK: Manchester University Press, 2004.
Zerafa, Peter Paul. "The Limits of Biblical Inerrancy." *For the Sake of Our Salvation: The Truth and Humility of God's Word. Letter & Spirit* 6 (2010) 359–76.

www.ingramcontent.com/pod-product-compliance
Lightning Source LLC
Chambersburg PA
CBHW072157160426
43197CB00012B/2419